First Hanon Exercises

The Virtuoso Pianist, Part 1 by C. L. Hanon (Abridged)

Plus 24 Major and Minor Scales, Chords, and Arpeggios

Edited by Keith Snell

The Virtuoso Pianist in 60 Exercises by C. L. Hanon (1819-1900) is probably the most popular piano technique book in history. *First Hanon Exercises* is an abridged version of the first 20 of Hanon's 60 exercises, making them useful for late elementary and early intermediate piano students. Eighth notes are used instead of sixteenth notes; each exercise has only 16 measures instead of 32; and the hands are placed two octaves apart for greater comfort. Scales, primary chord progressions, and tonic chord arpeggios are included in all twenty-four keys. Chromatic scales also add to the usefulness of this book.

These time-tested exercises greatly enhance the development of finger dexterity, coordination, and evenness of touch.

CONTENTS

HANON EXERCISES 1-20	2-21
MAJOR SHARP SCALES	22
MAJOR FLAT SCALES	23
MINOR SHARP SCALES	24
MINOR FLAT SCALES	25
PRIMARY CHORD PROGRESSIONS	
Major Sharp Keys	26
Major Flat Keys	27
Minor Sharp Keys	28
Minor Flat Keys	29
TONIC CHORD ARPEGGIOS	
12 Major Keys	30
12 Minor Keys	31
CHROMATIC SCALES	32

ISBN-10: 0-8497-9862-0
ISBN-13: 978-0-8497-9862-7

©2019 Neil A. Kjos Music Company, 4382 Jutland Drive, San Diego, California 92117.
International copyright secured. All rights reserved. Printed in the U.S.A.
Warning! The contents of this publication are protected by copyright law. To copy or reproduce them by any method is an infringement of the copyright law. Anyone who reproduces copyrighted matter is subject to substantial penalties and assessments for each infringement.

1.

Learn to play each exercise *legato* and **mf**. Next, practice each exercise with a variety of dynamics, articulations, and rhythm patterns to enhance technical development. Notated variants are available for free via a link on the Hanon First Exercises (GP562) product page at **Kjos.com**. All repeats are optional.

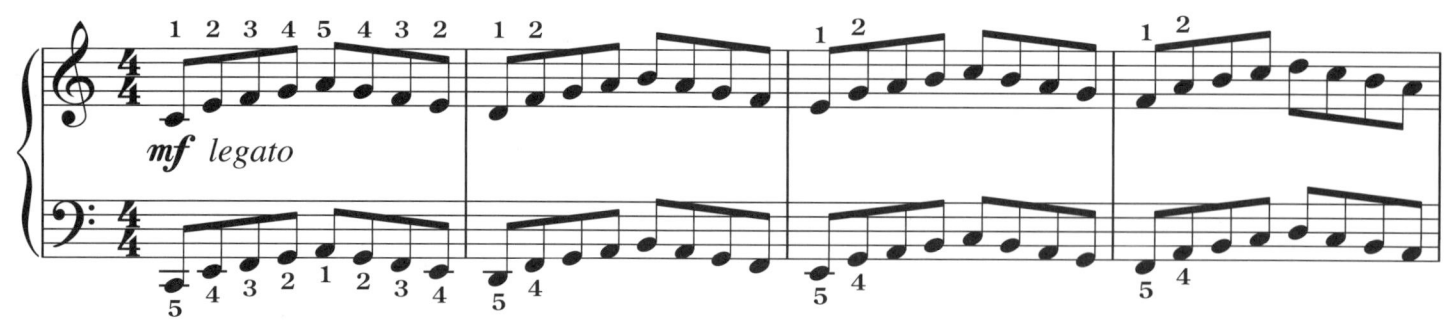

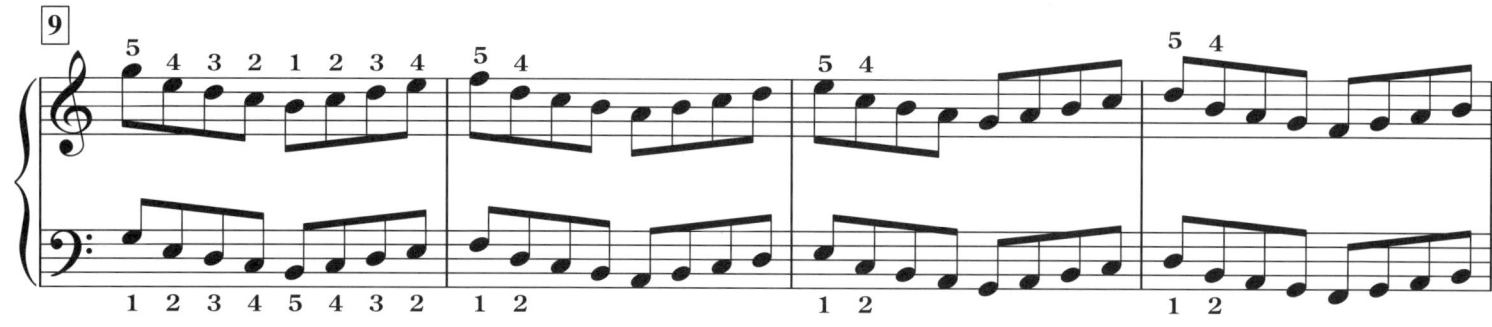

Once each exercise is mastered, you may:

  *omit measure 8 and proceed directly from measure 7 to 9 without stopping.

  **repeat from the end of measure 15, rather than 16.

2.

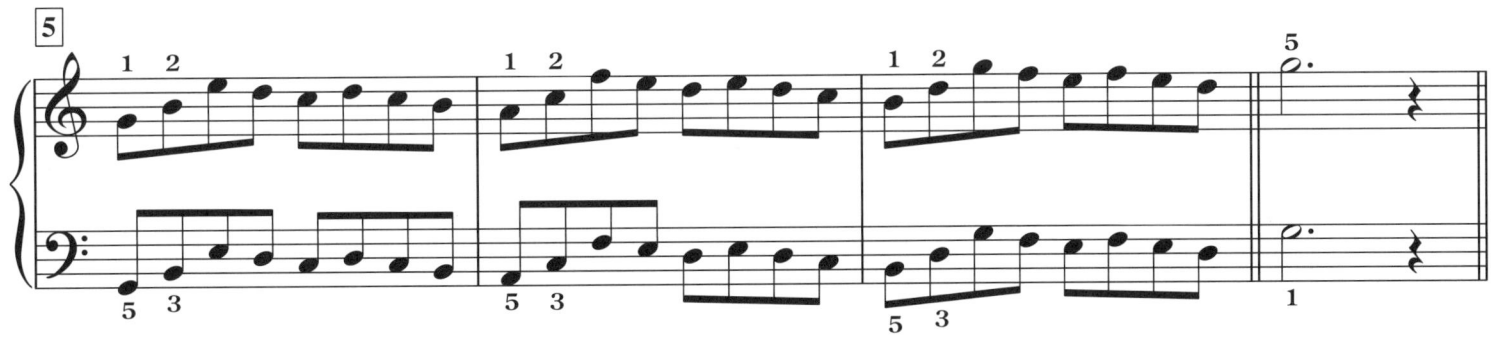
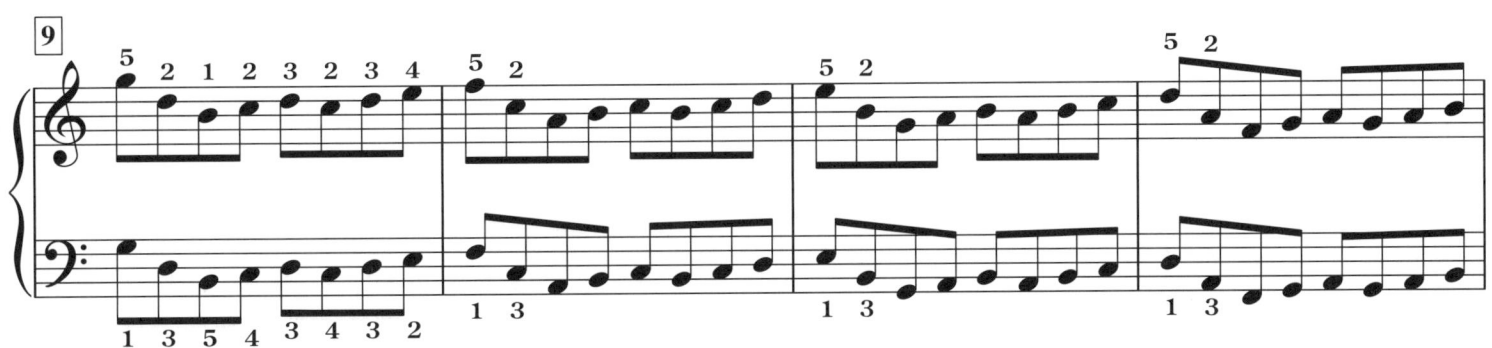
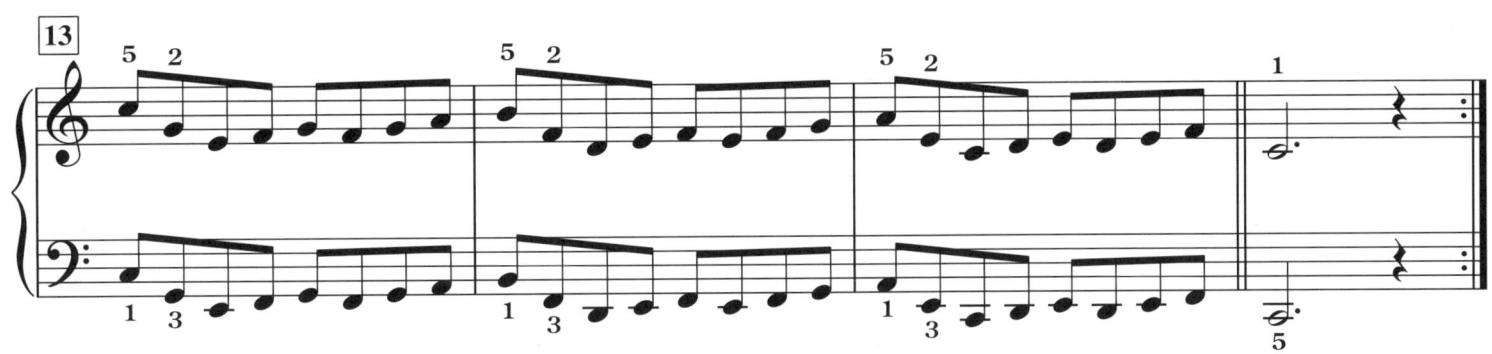

3.

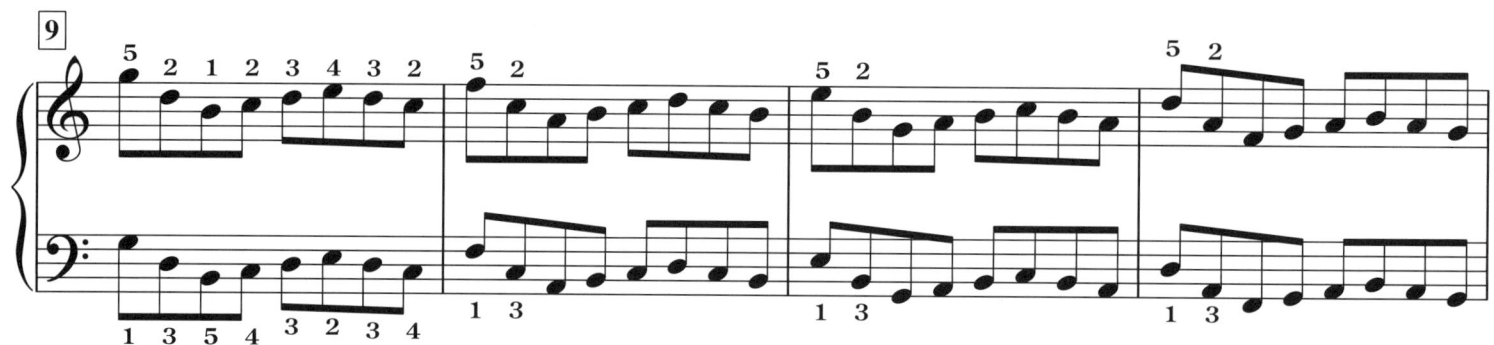

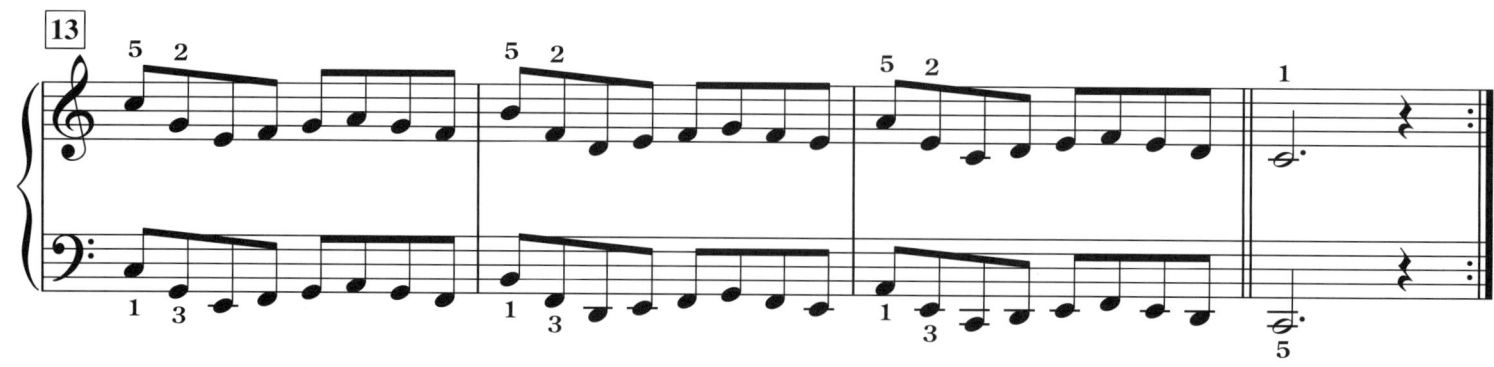

4.

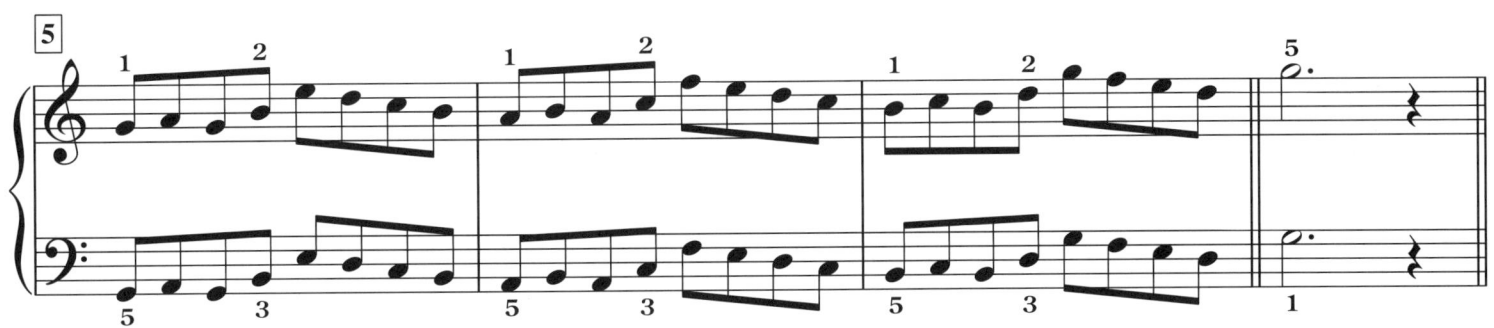
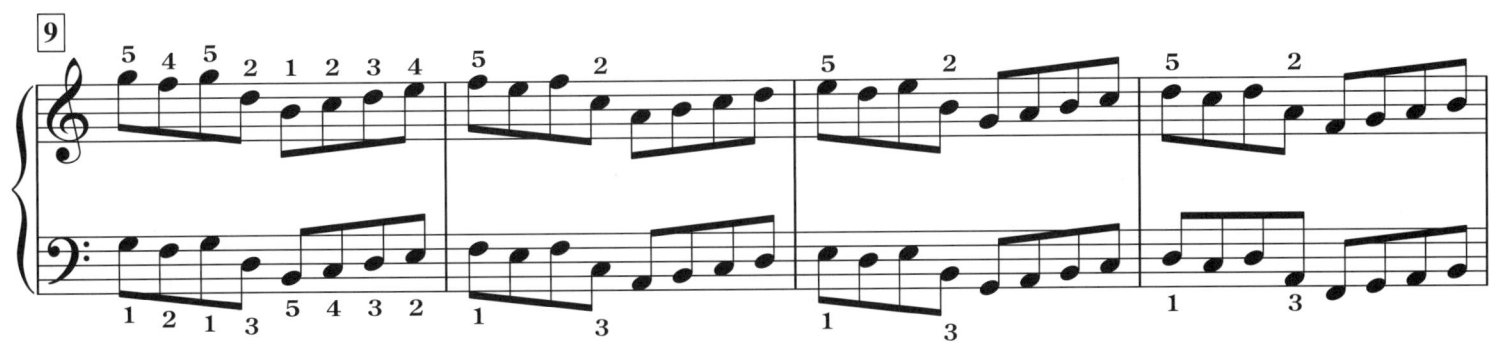

5.

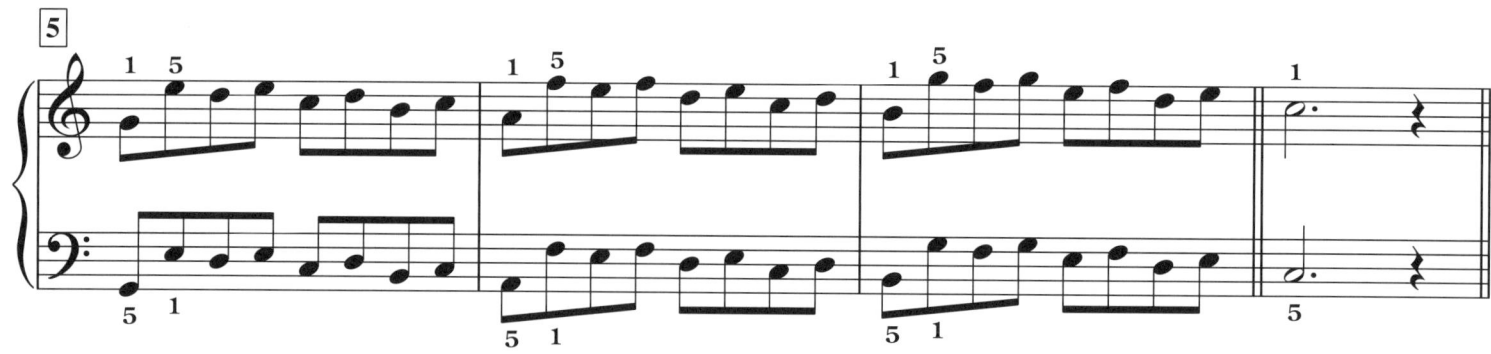
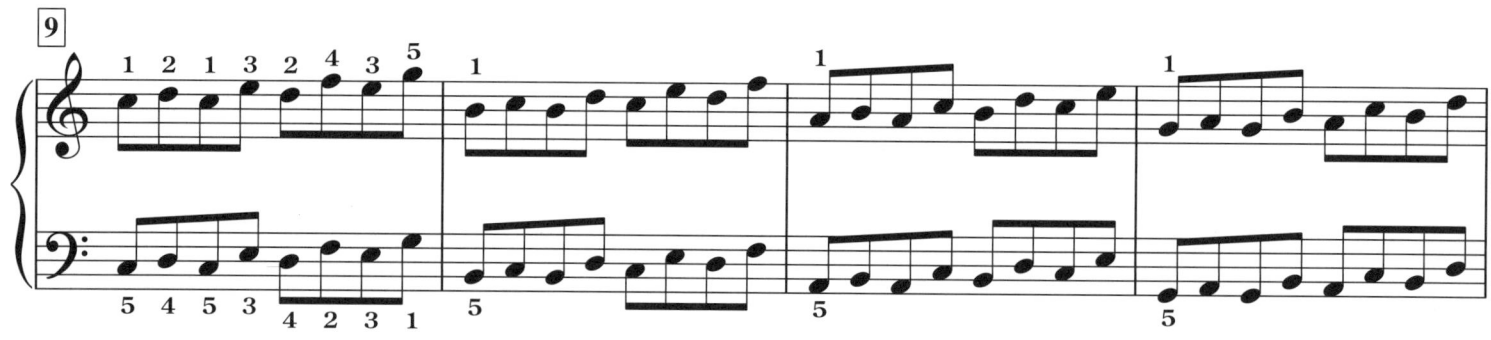

6.

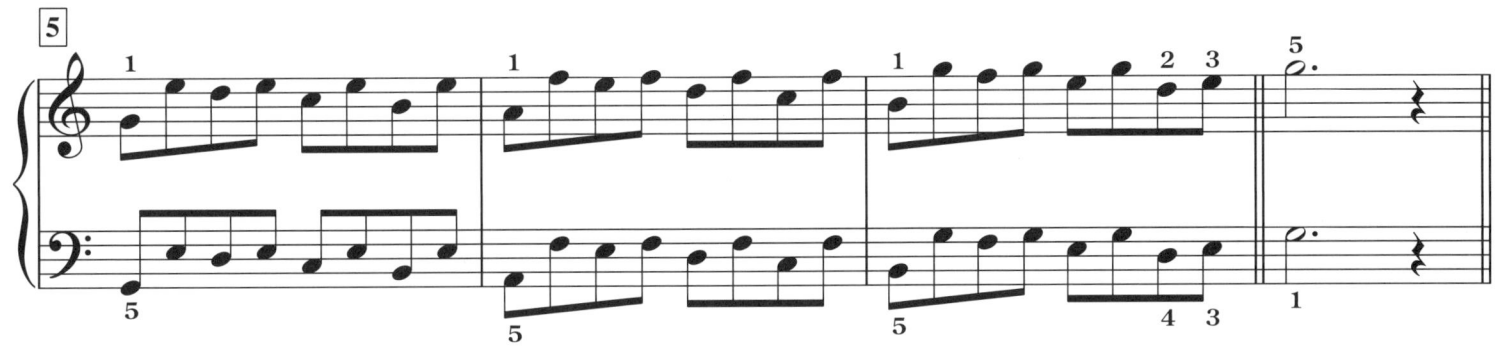
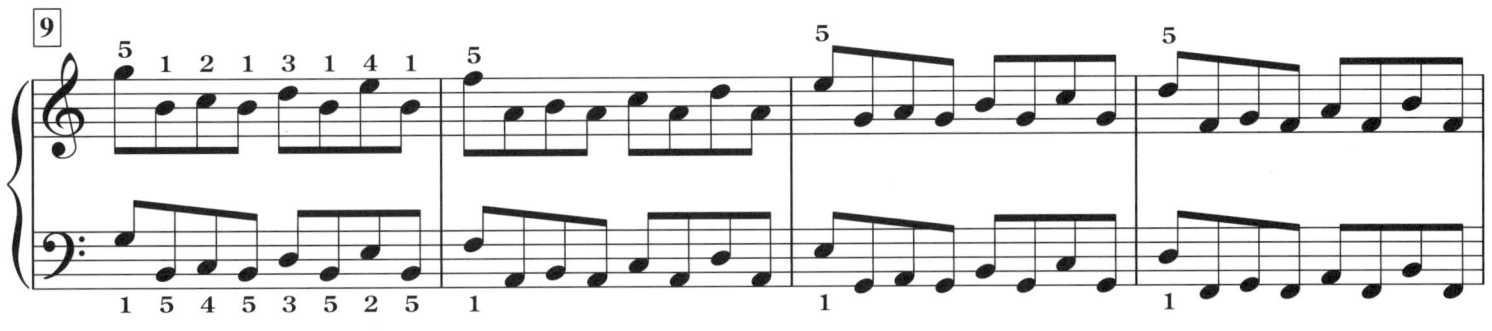
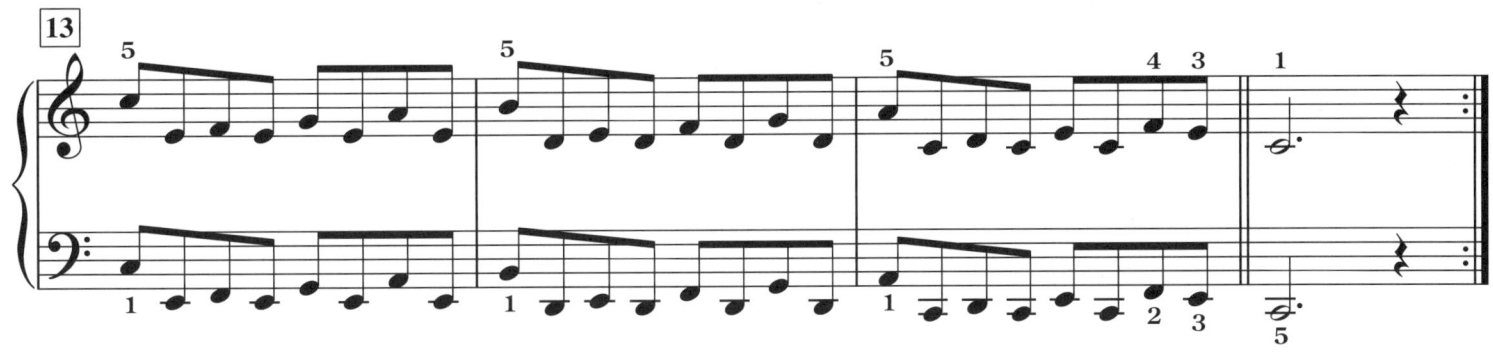

7.

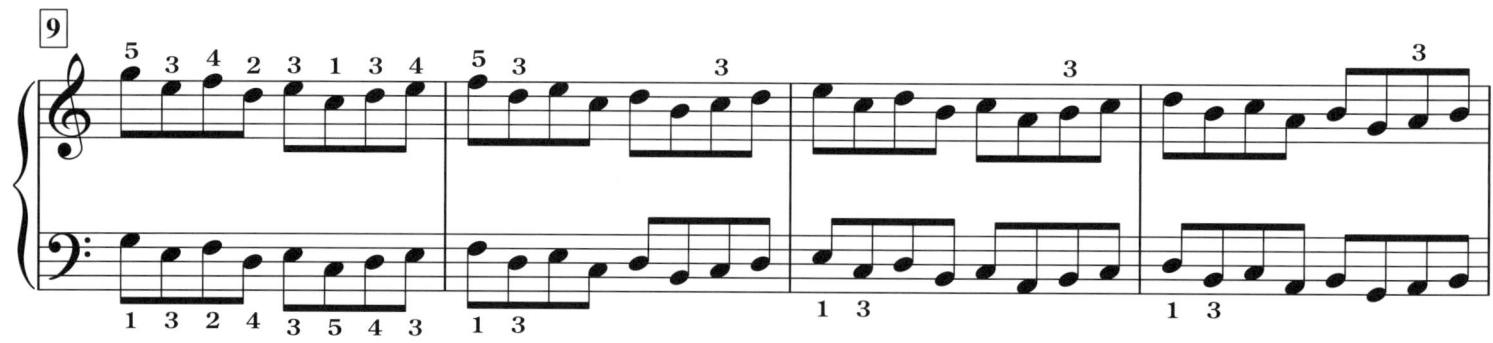
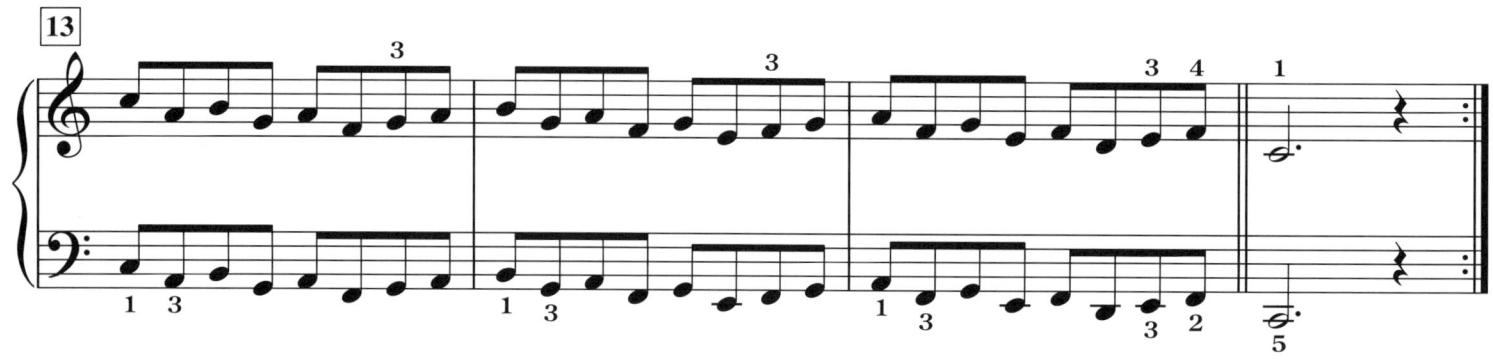

8.

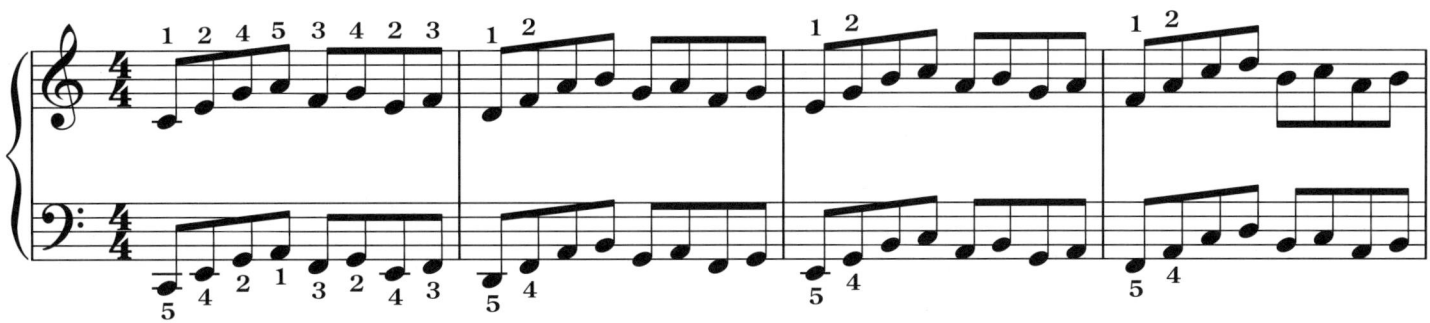

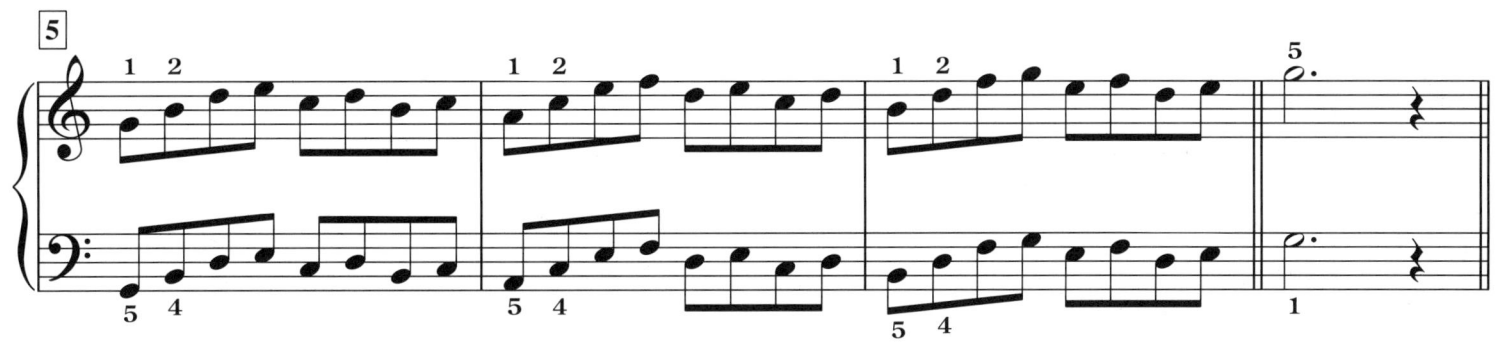

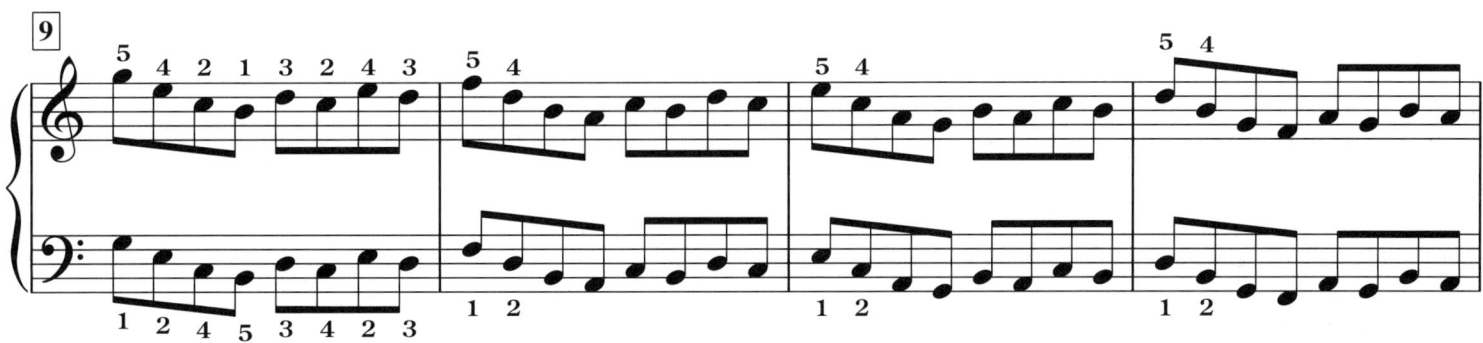

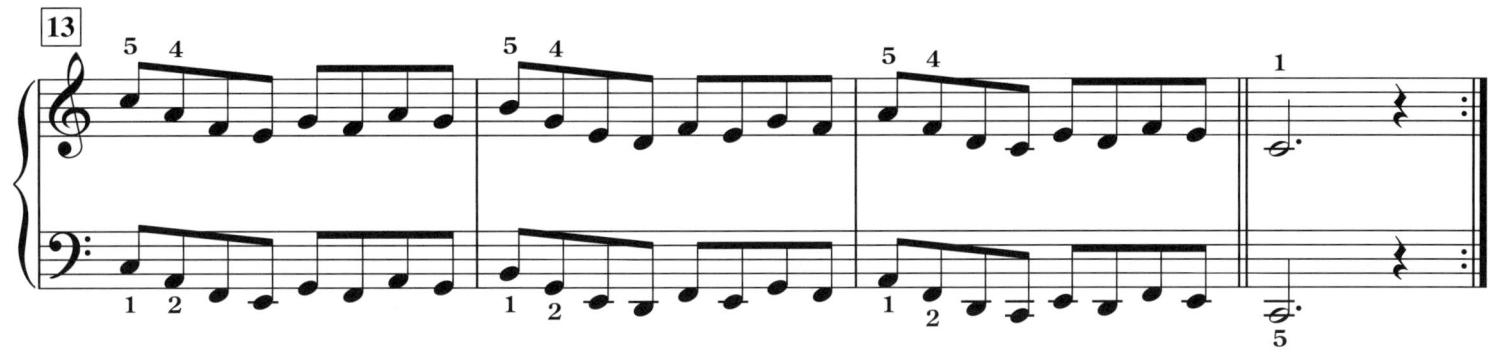

9.

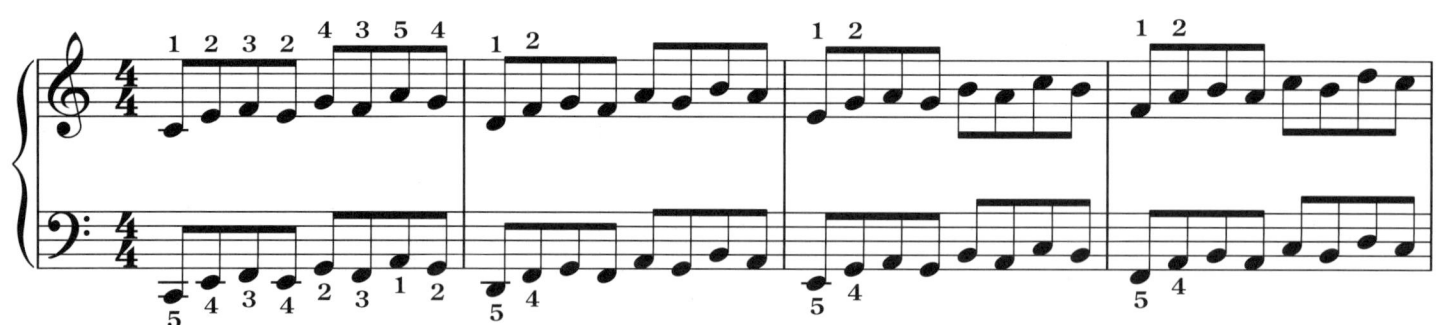

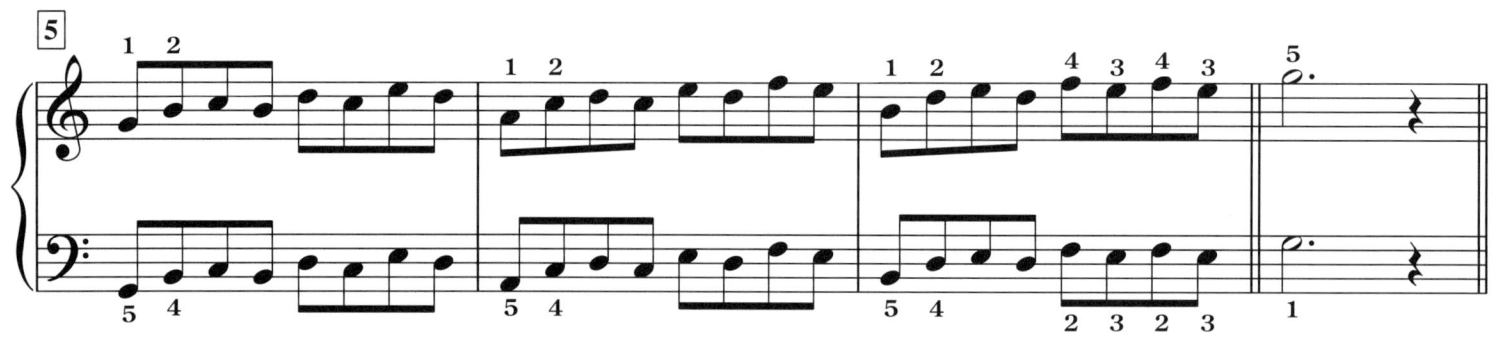

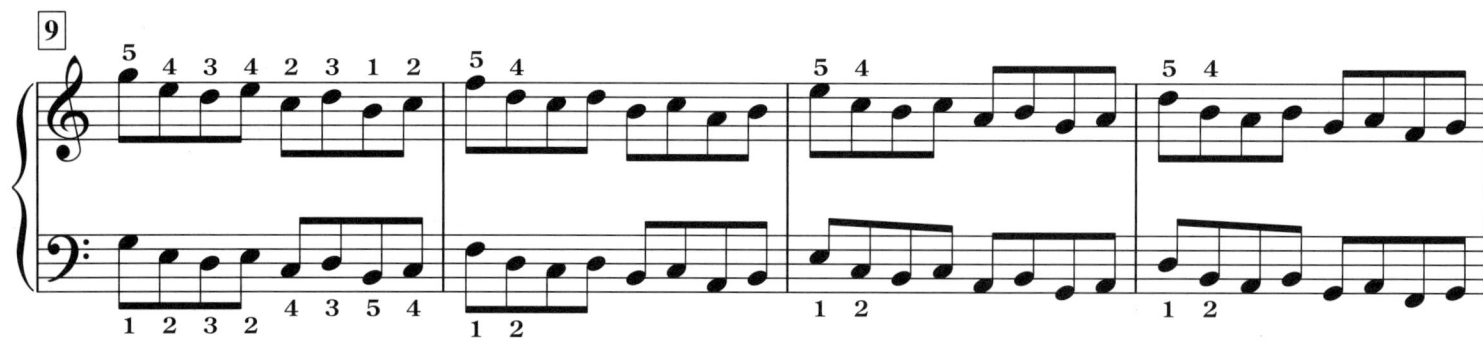

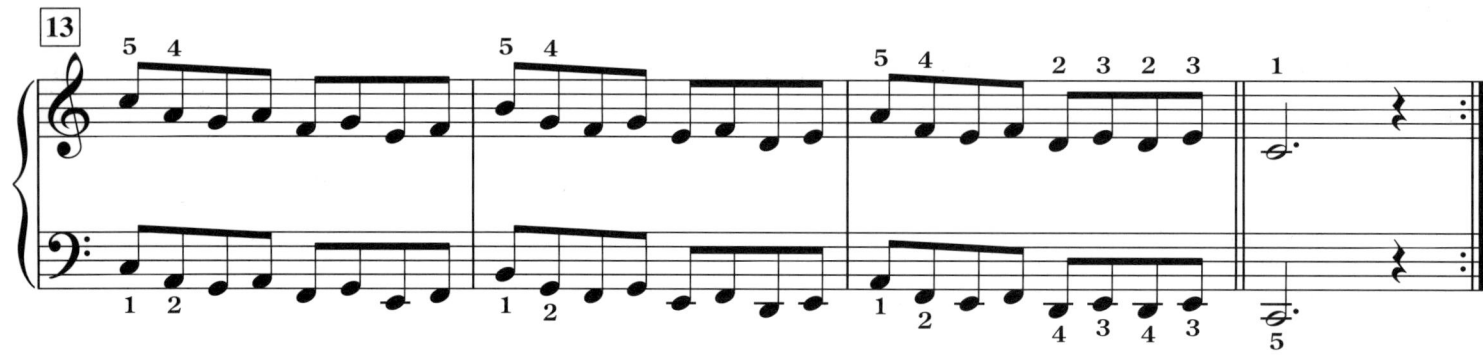

10.

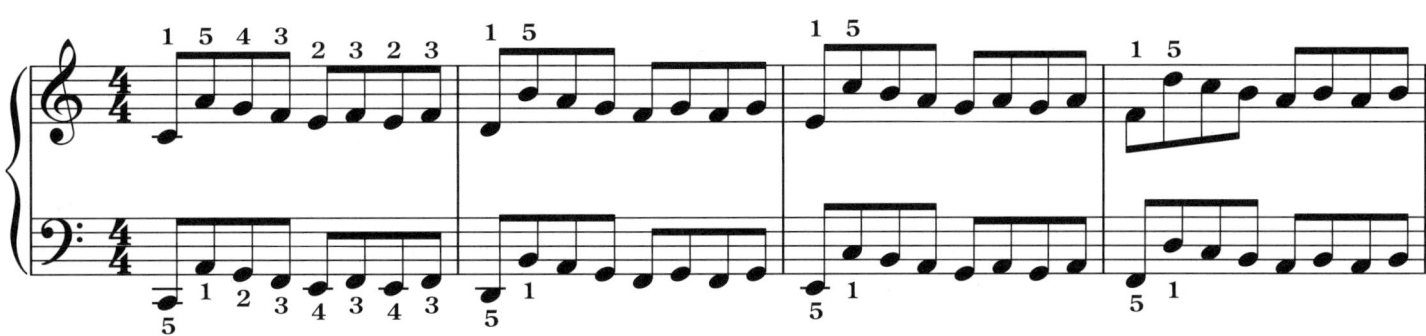
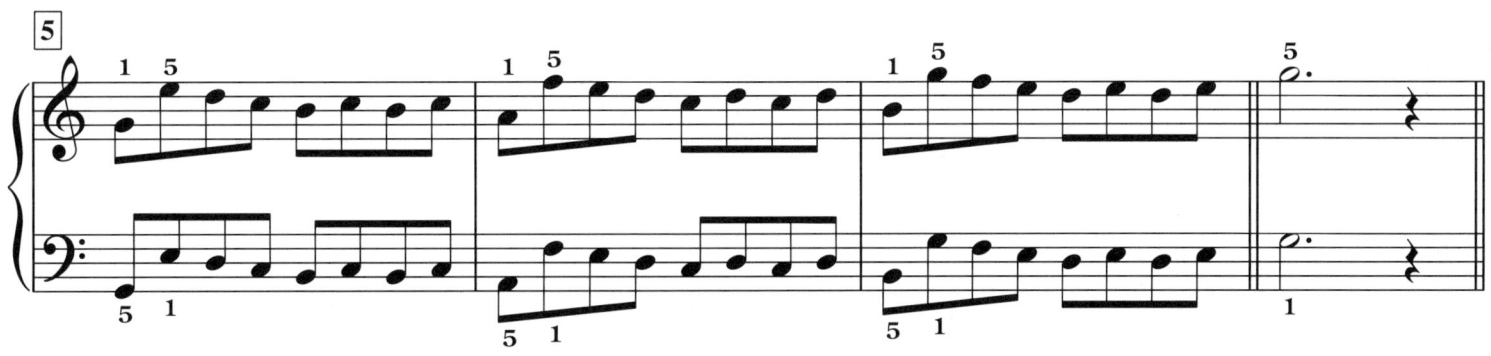
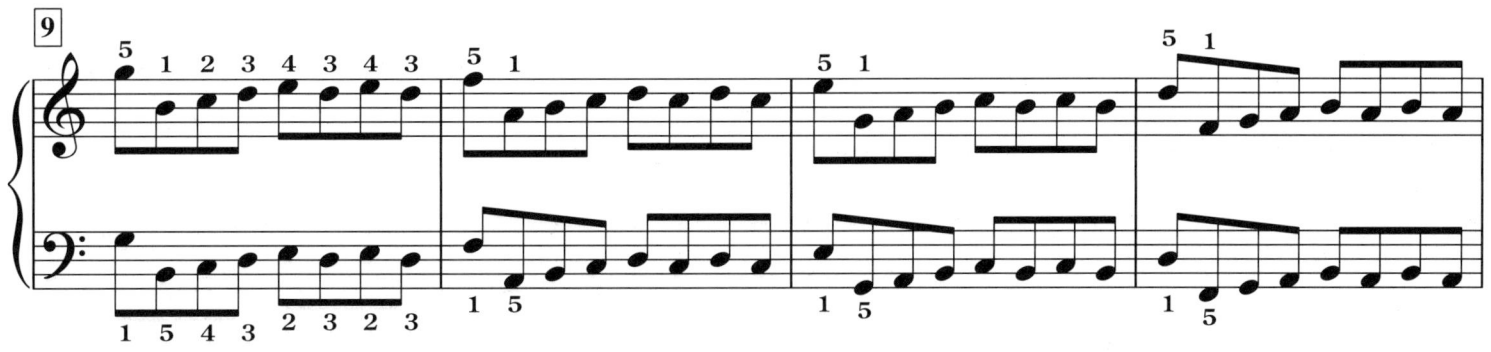
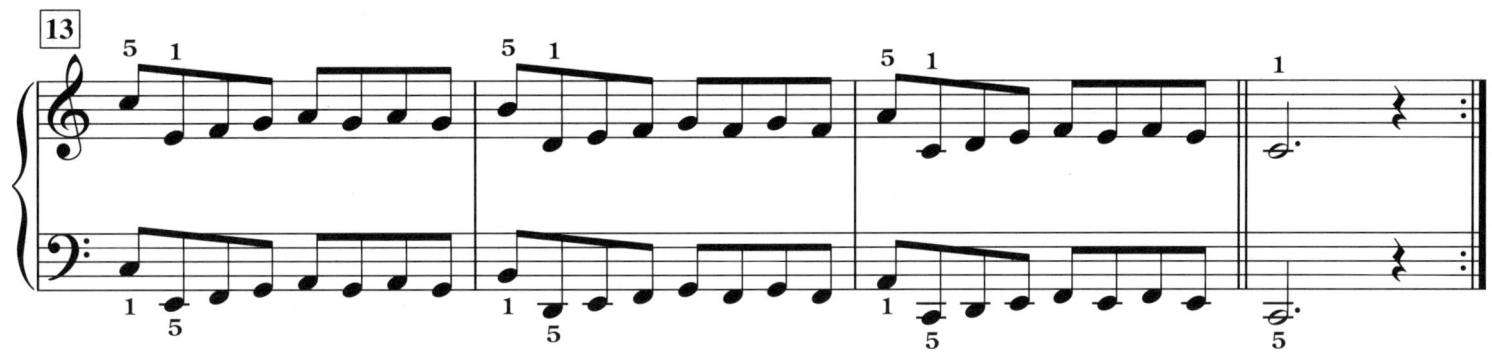

11.

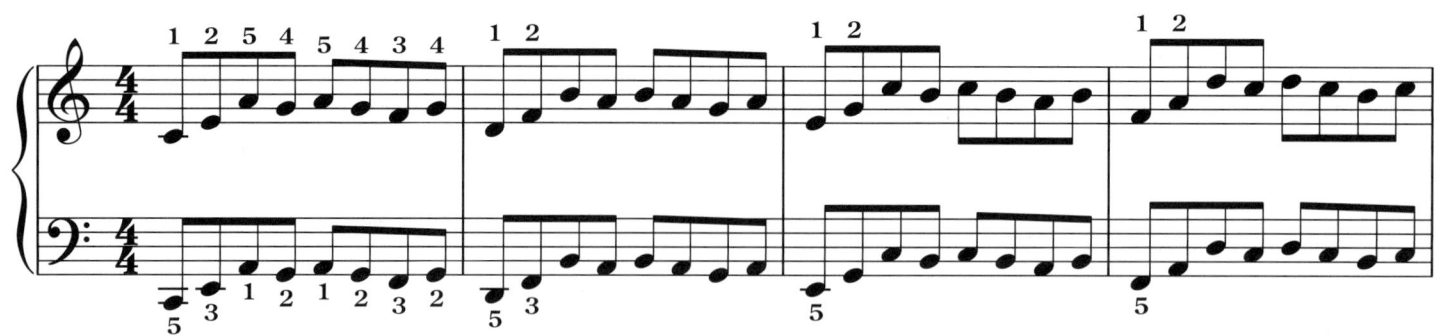
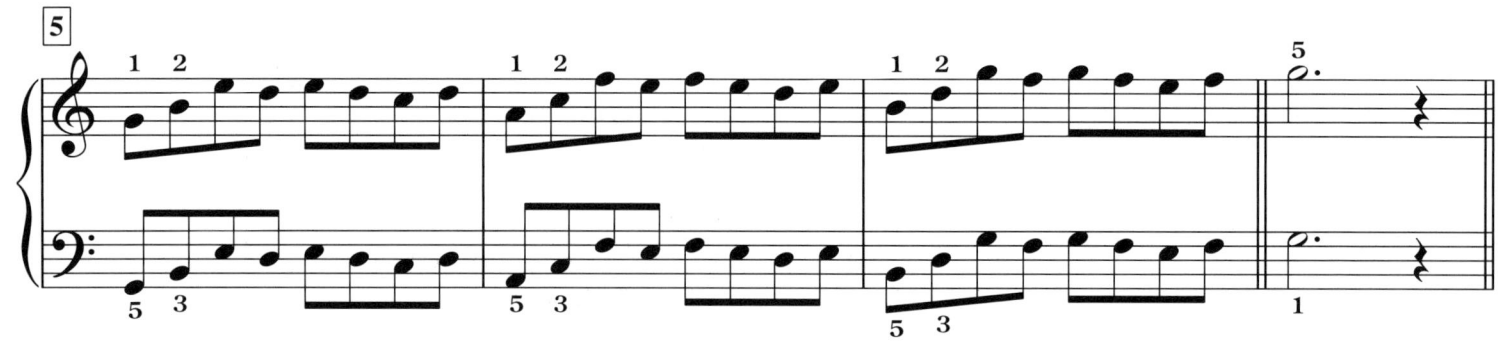
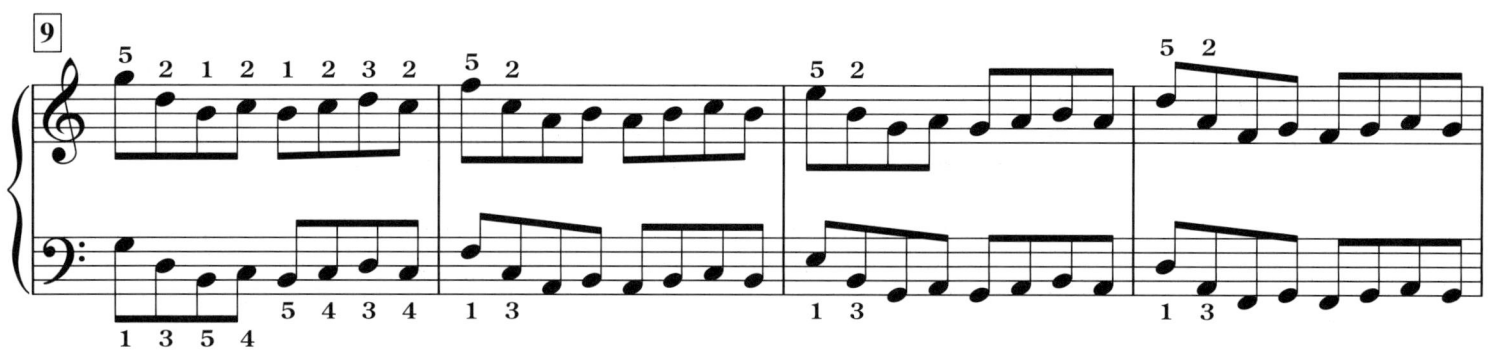
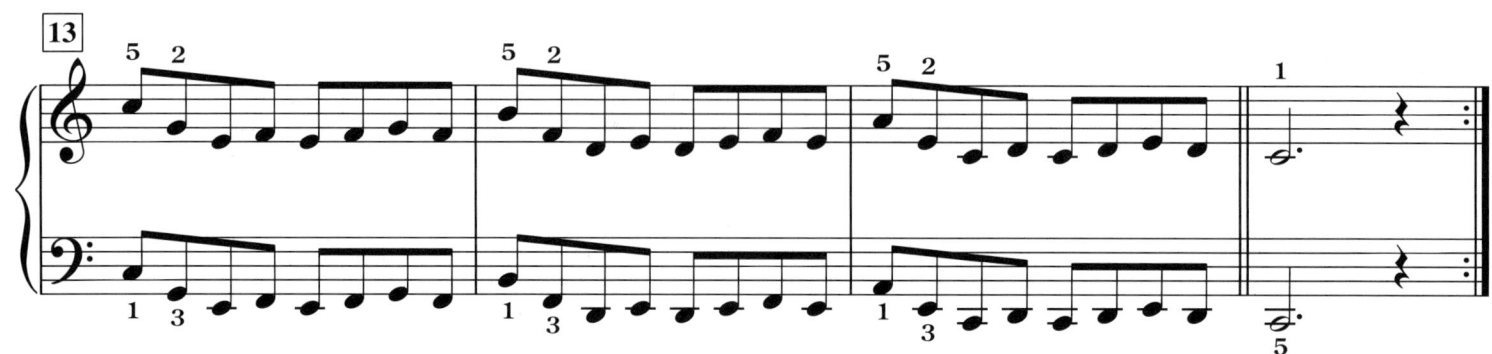

12.

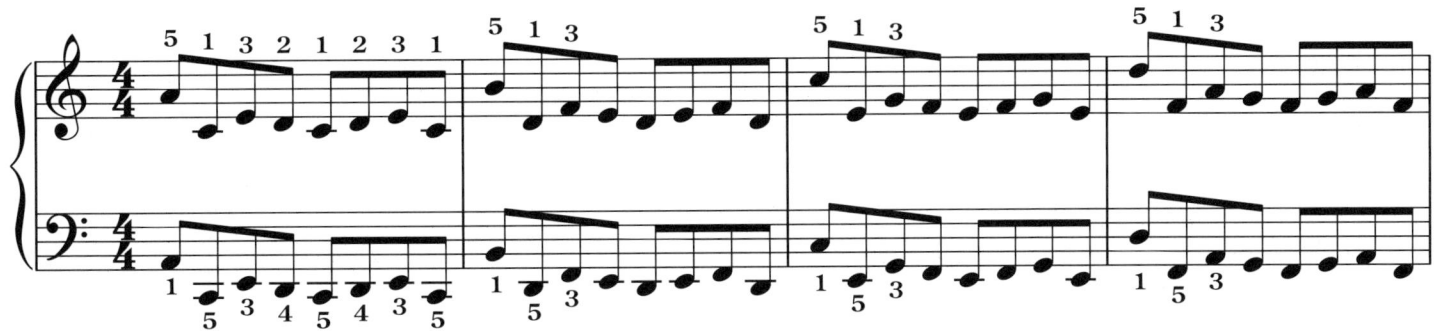

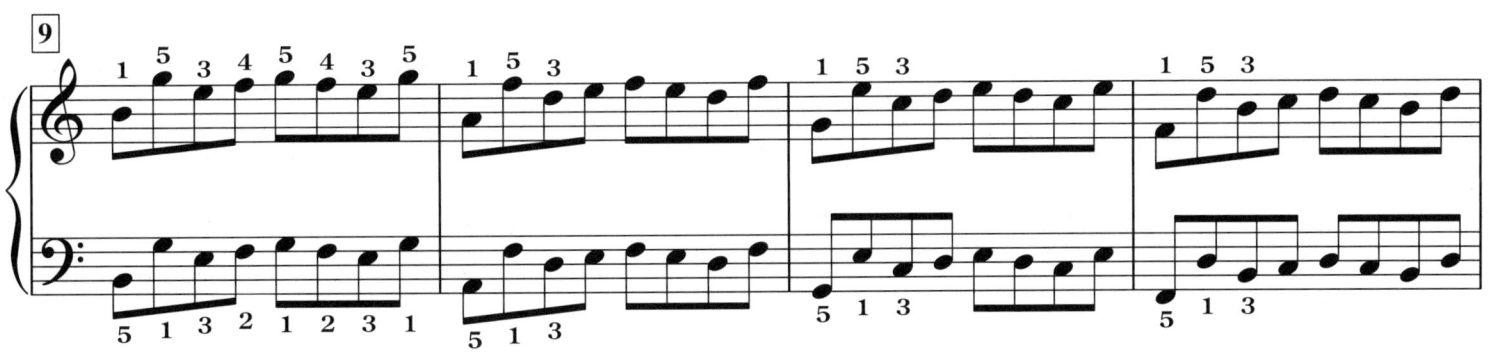

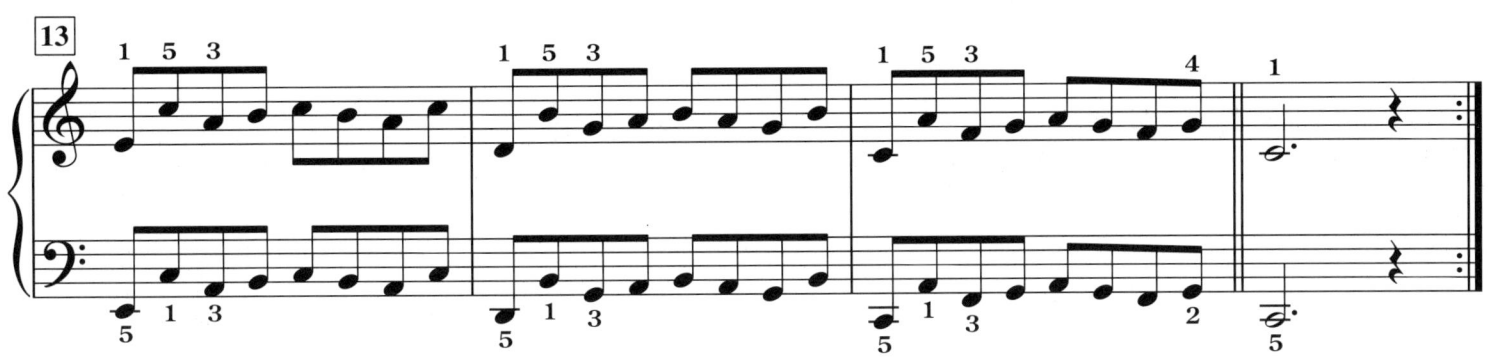

13.

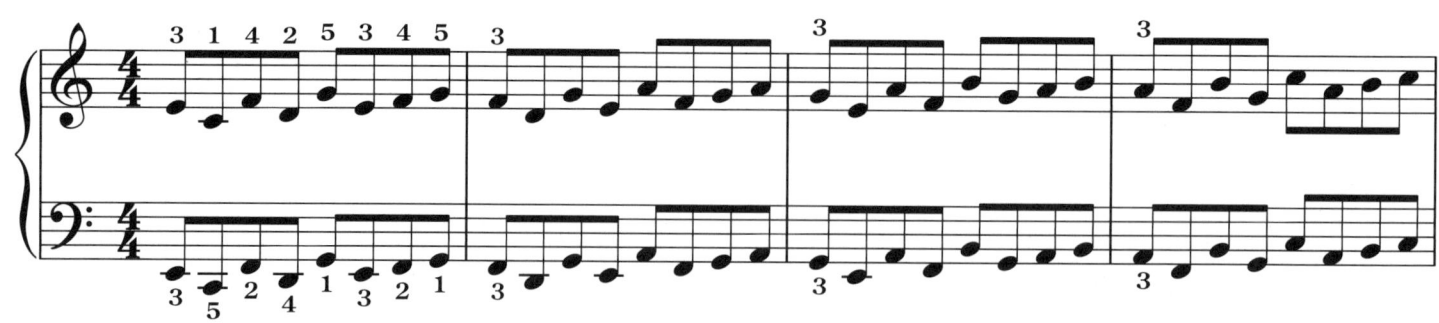

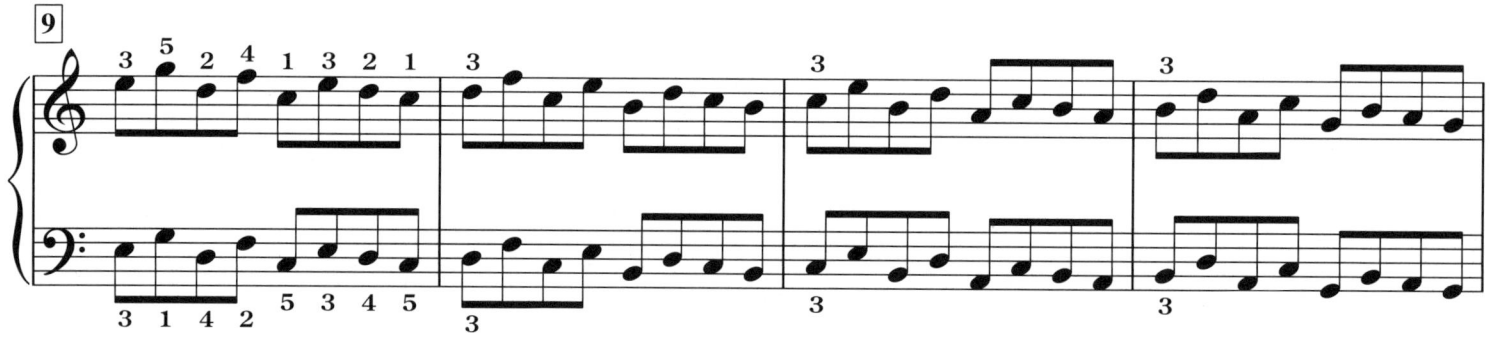

14.

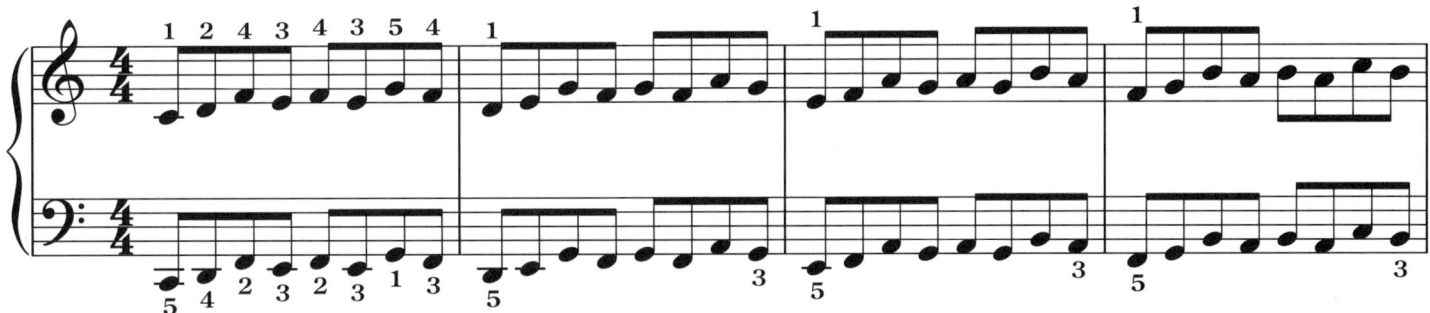
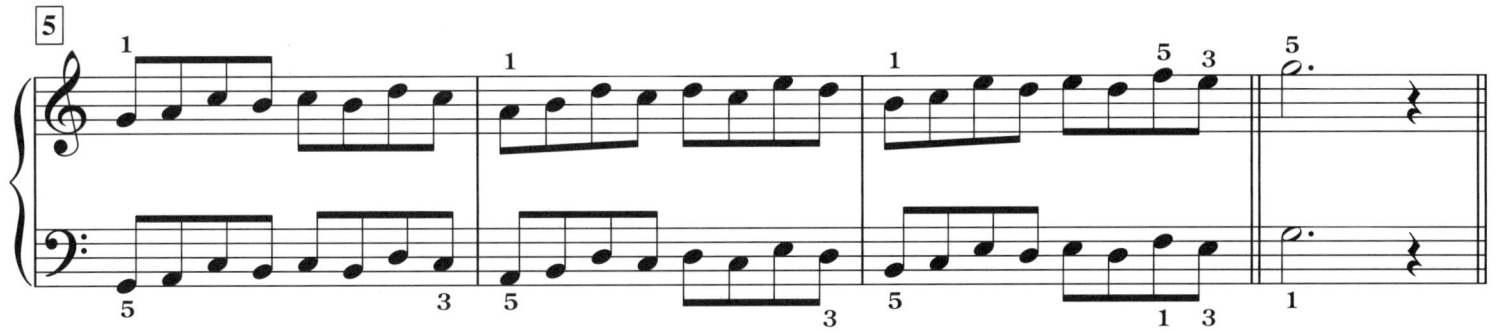

15.

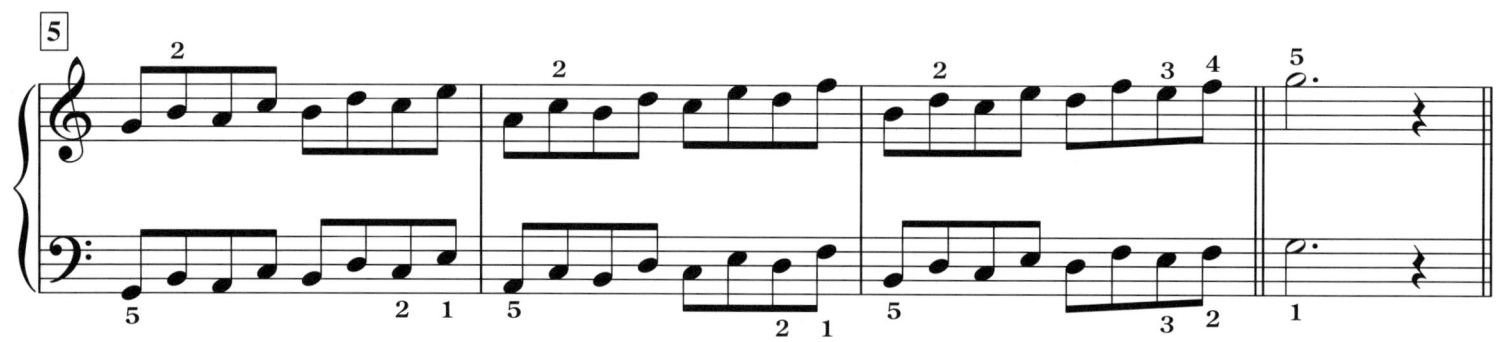
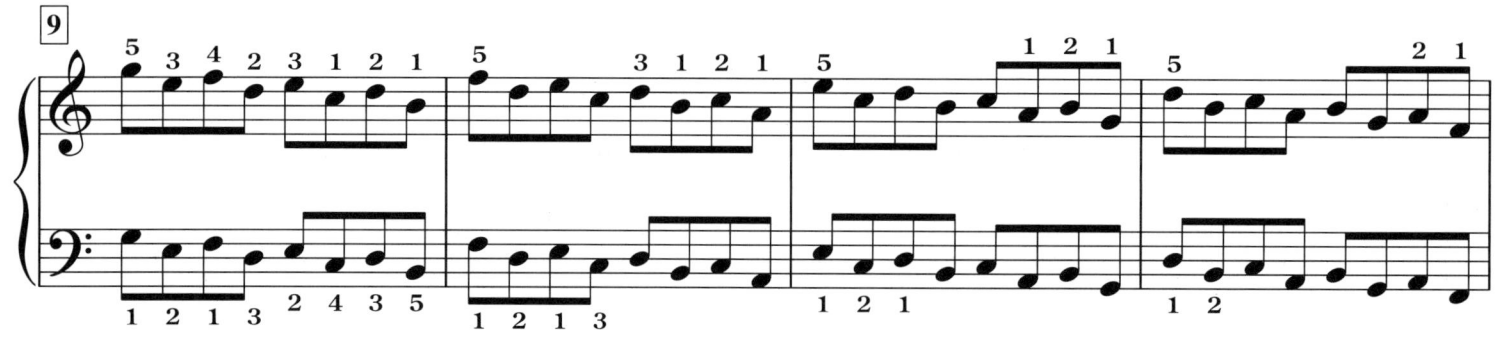
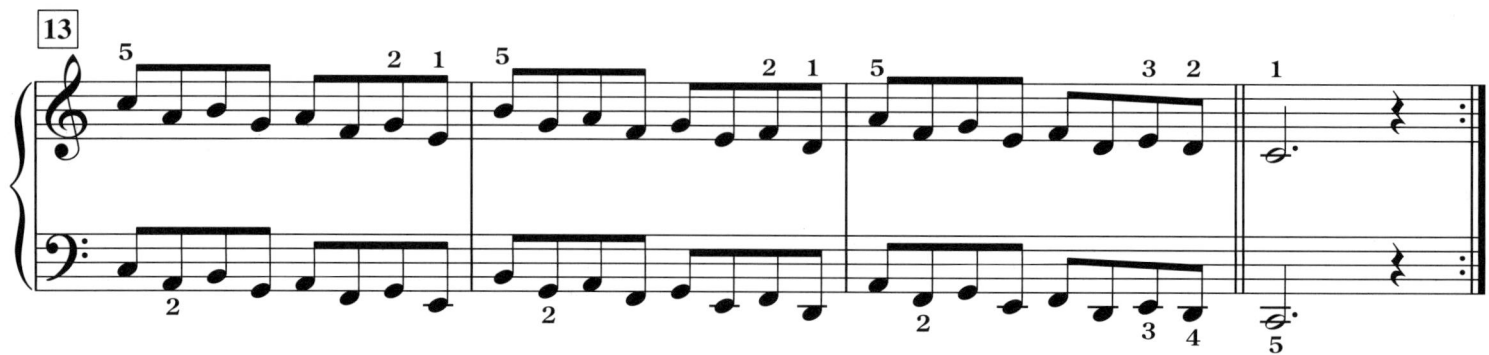

16.

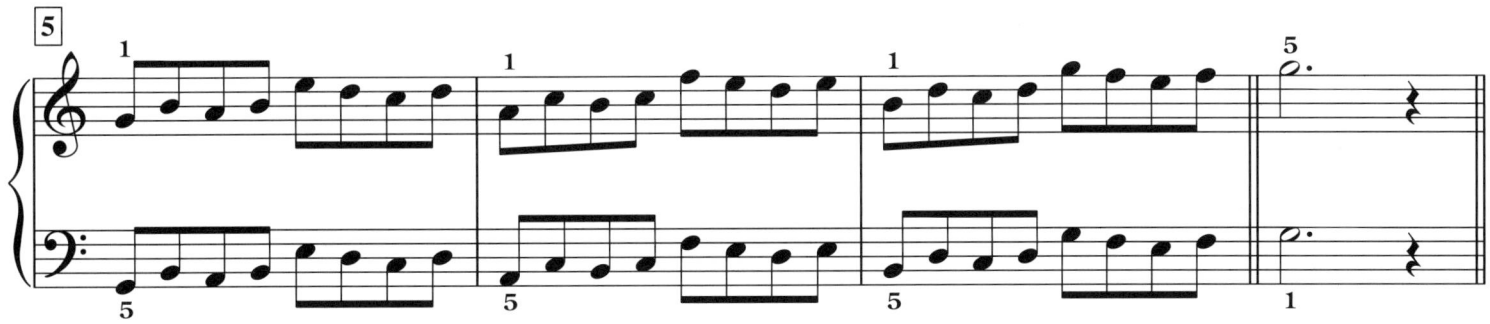
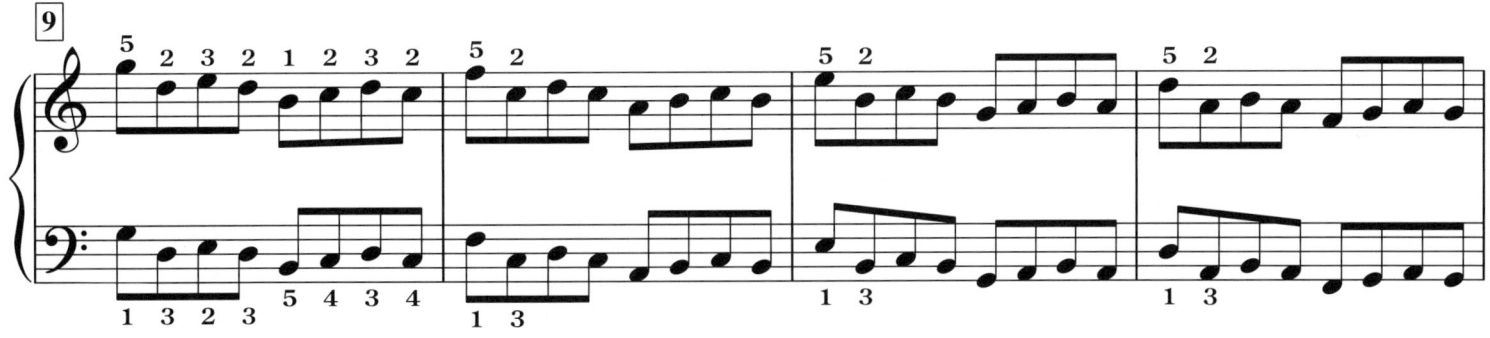
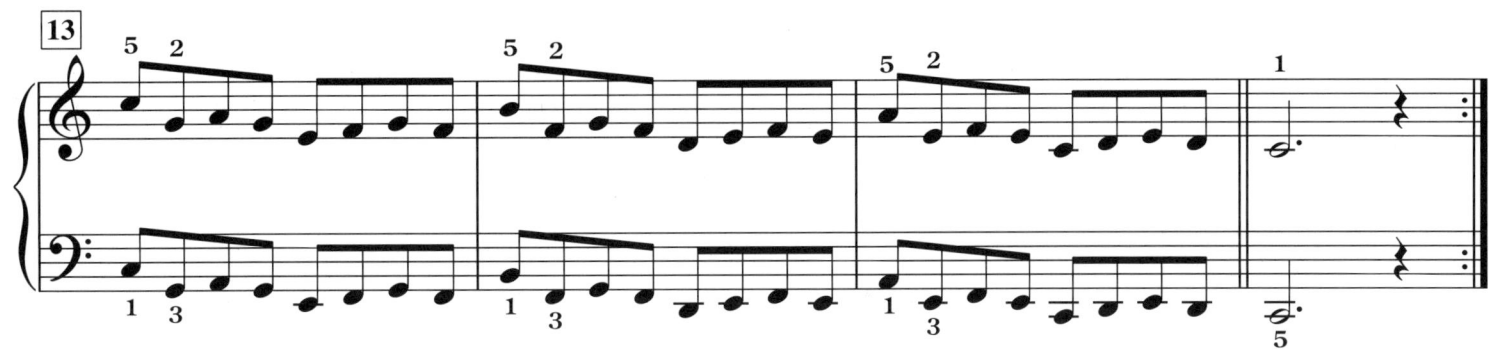

17.

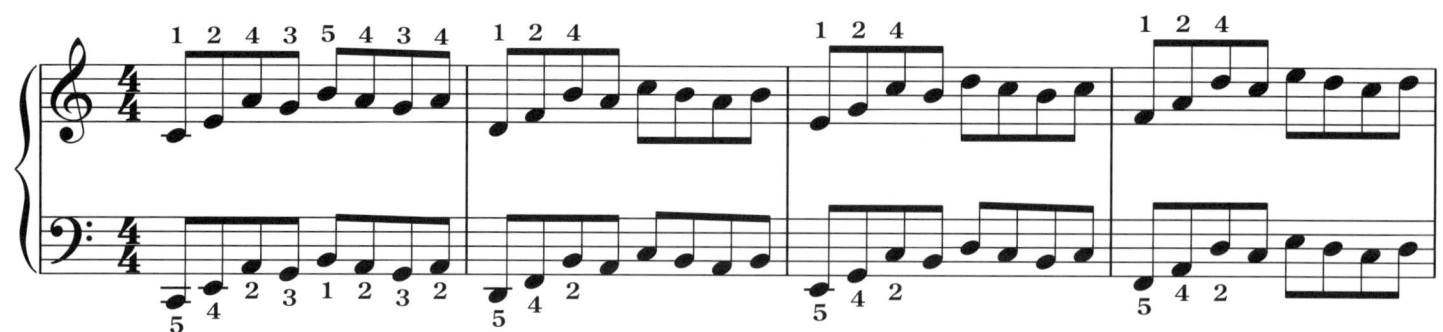
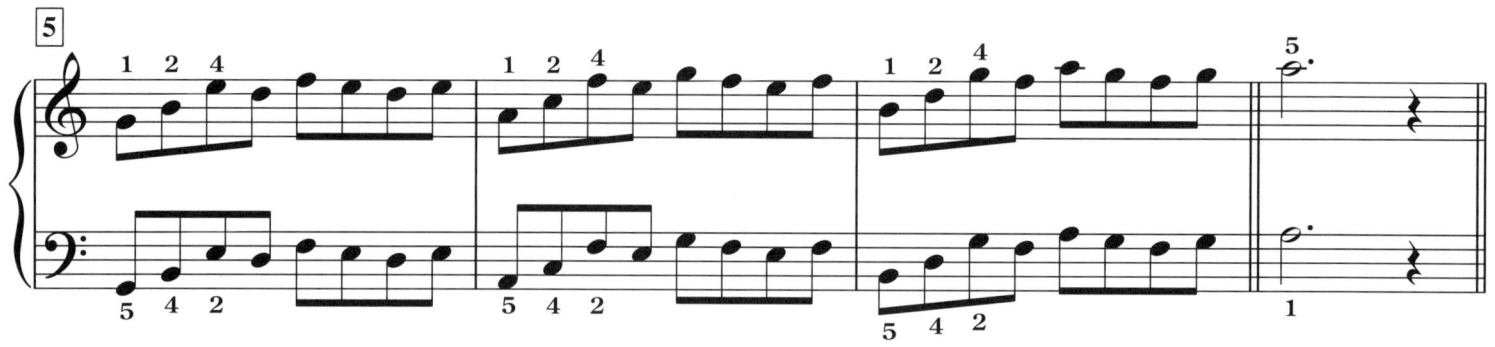
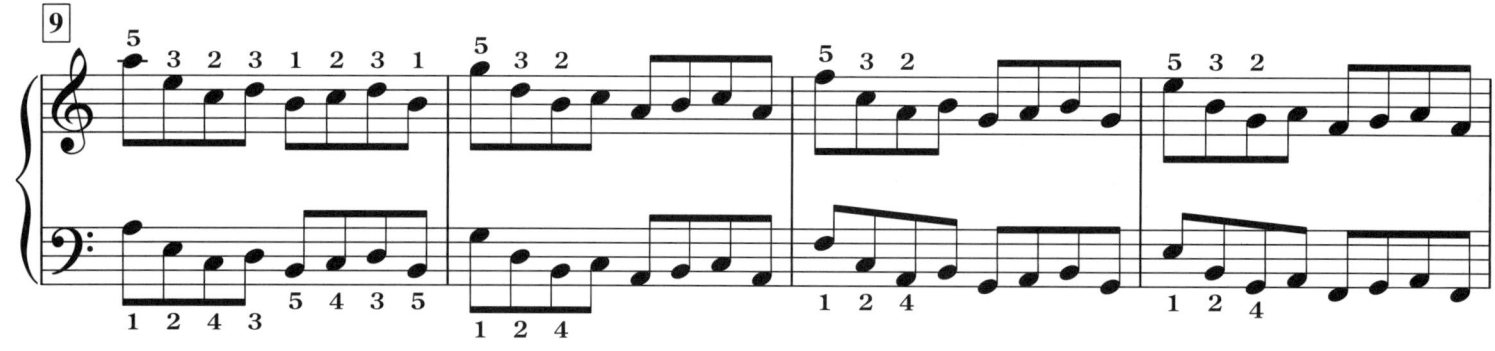
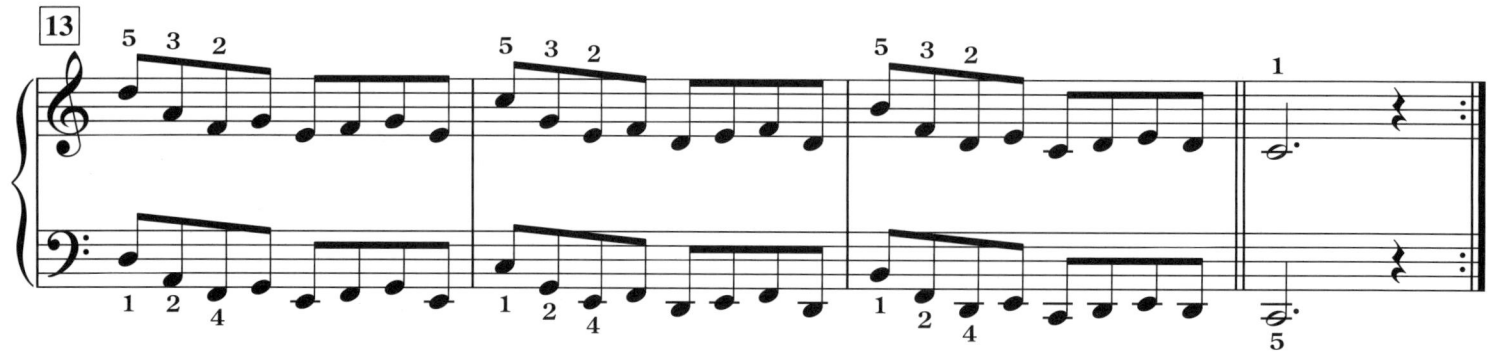

18.

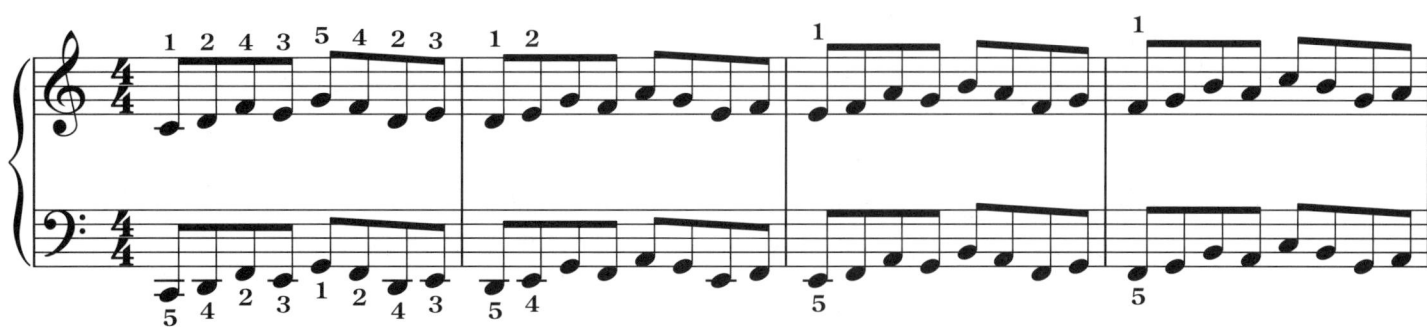
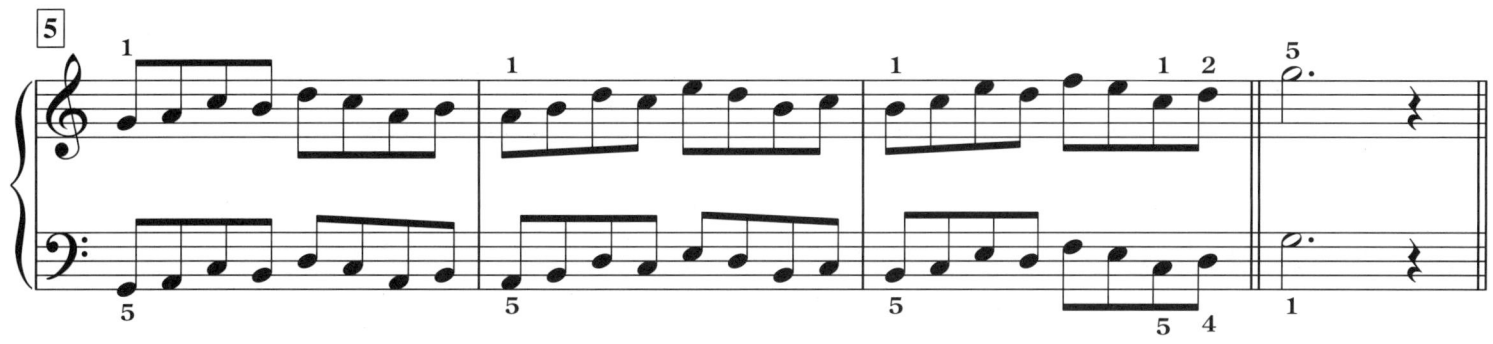
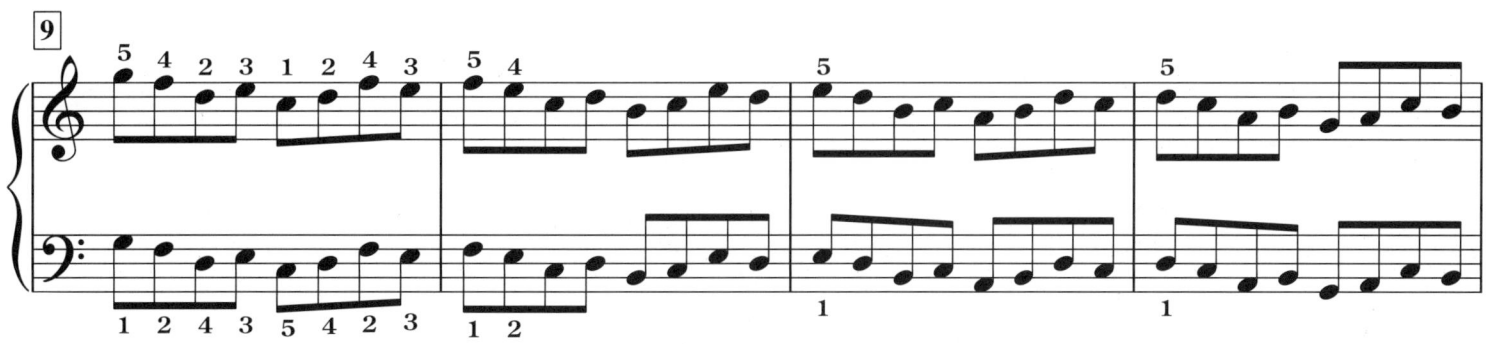
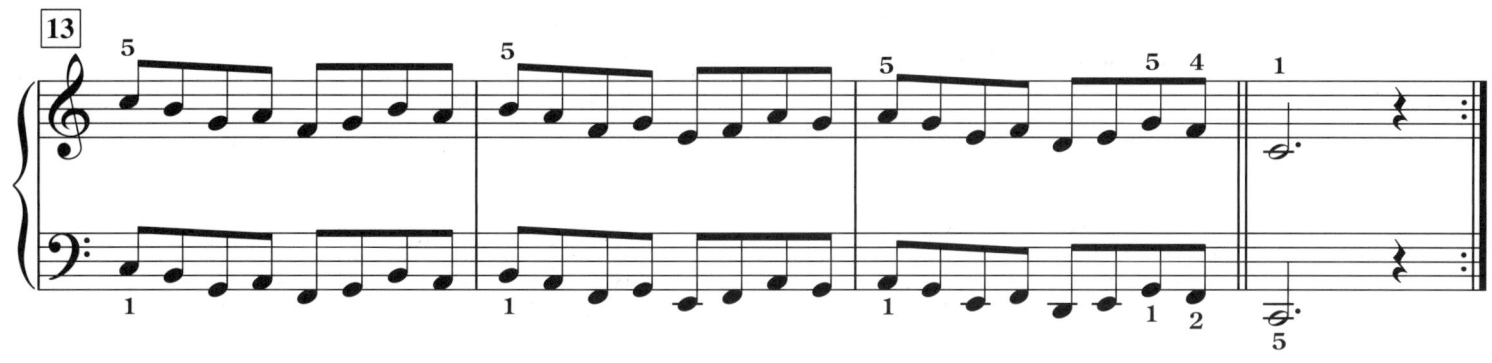

19.

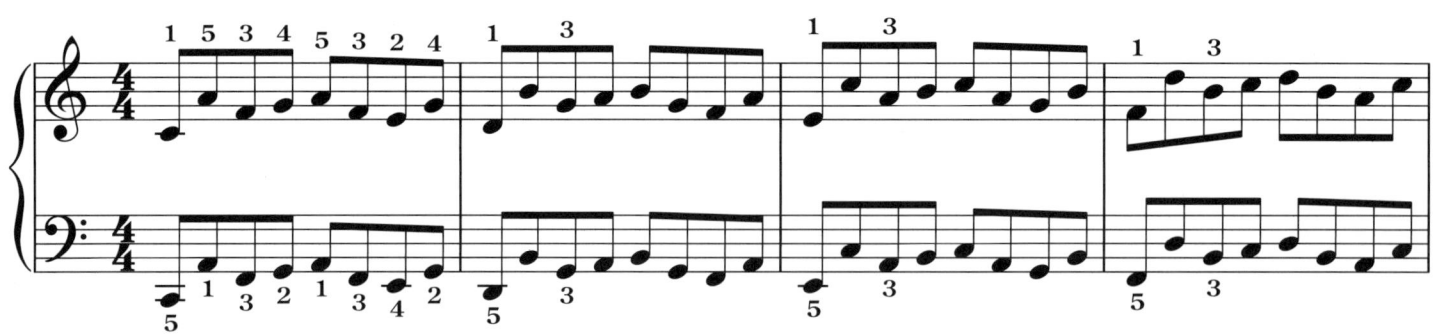
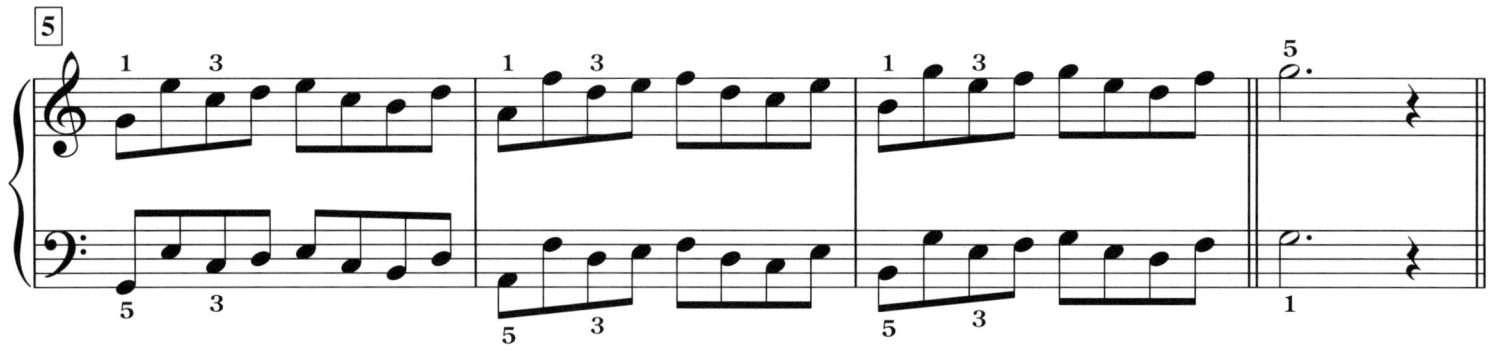
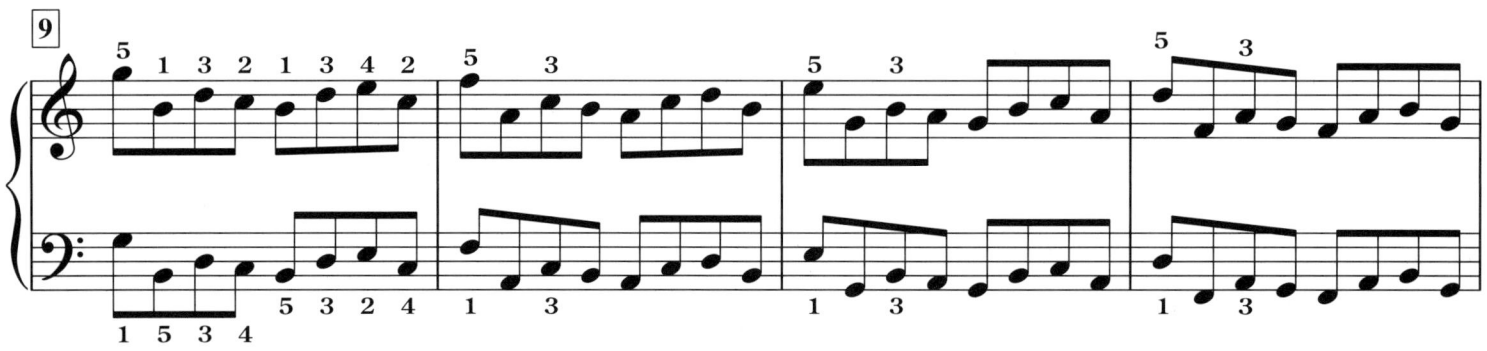
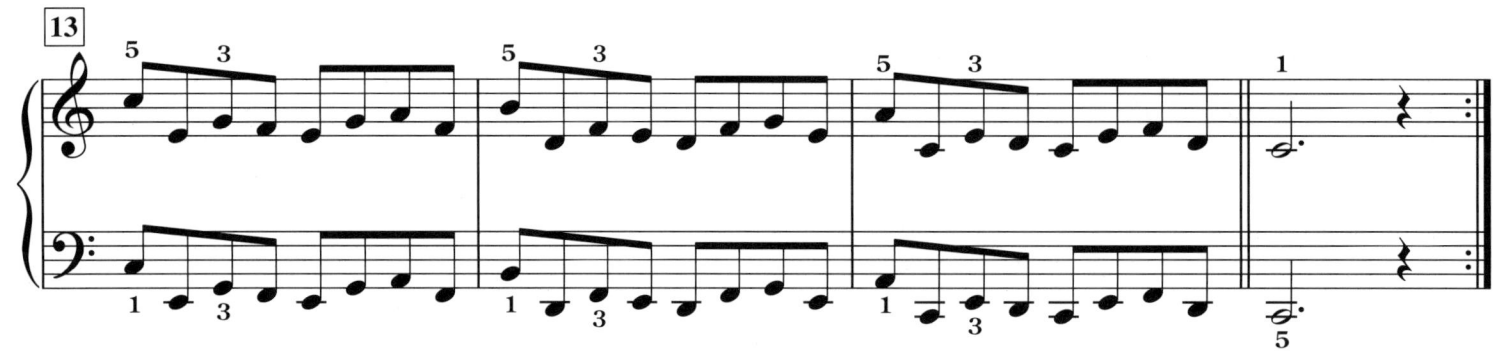

20.

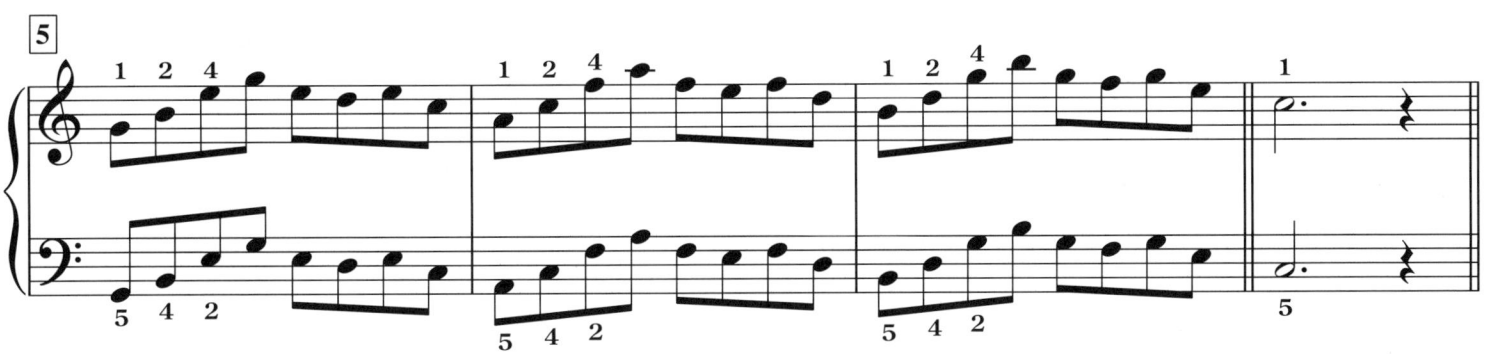
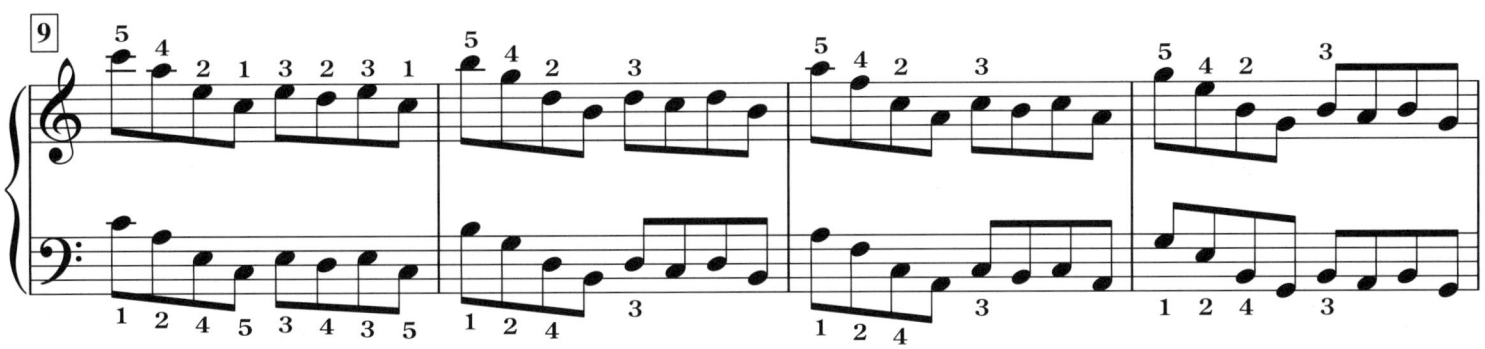
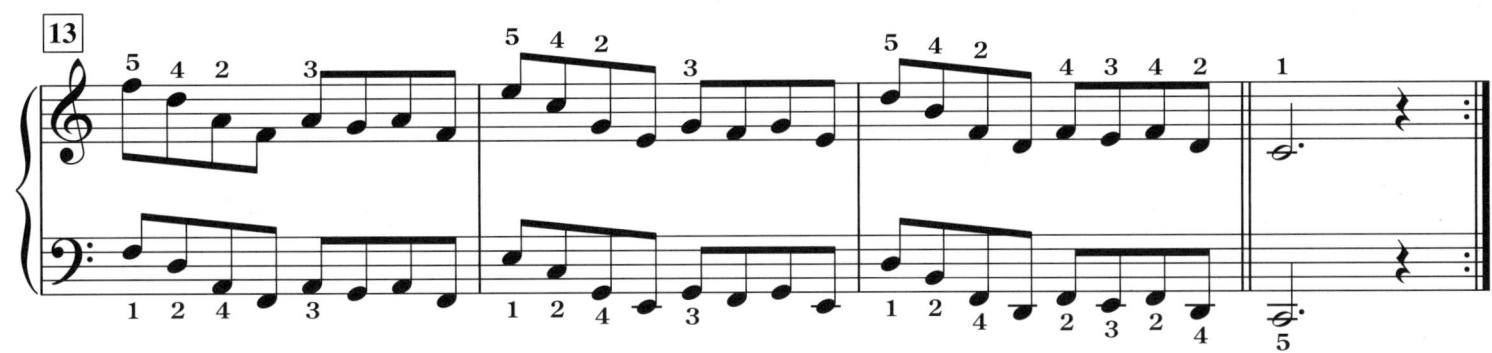

Major Sharp Scales

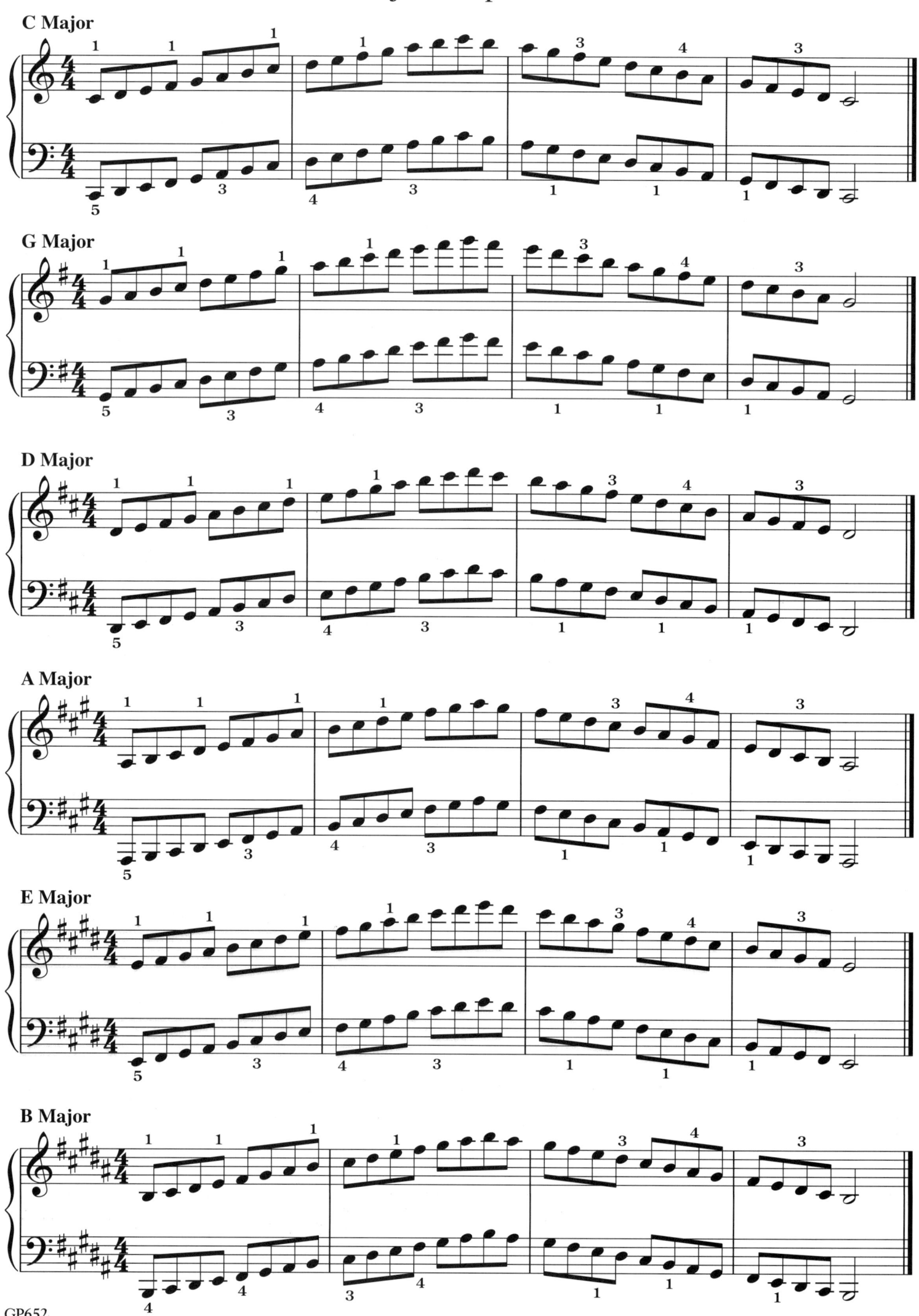

Major Flat Scales

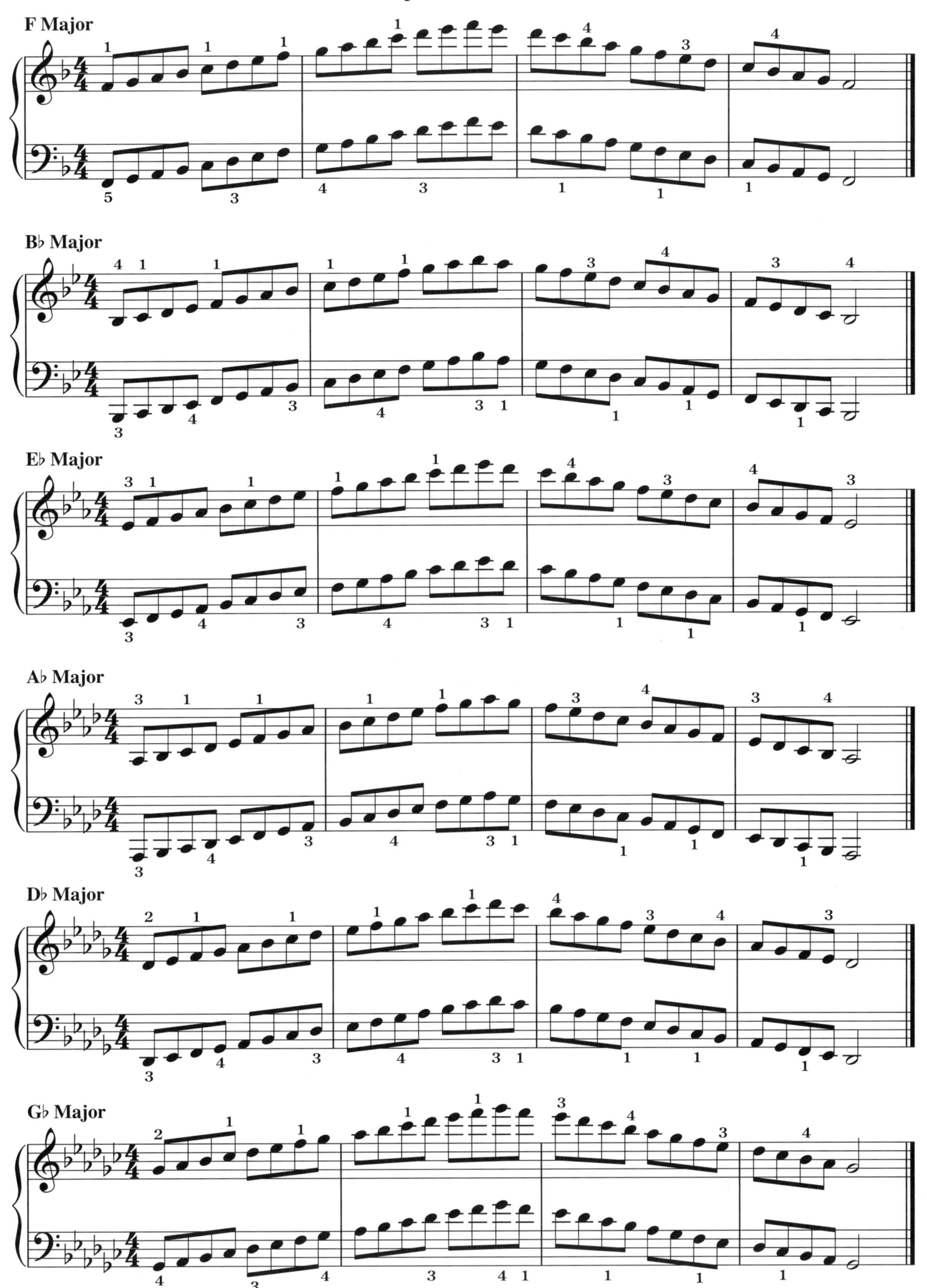

Minor Sharp Scales (Harmonic Form)

Minor Flat Scales (Harmonic Form)

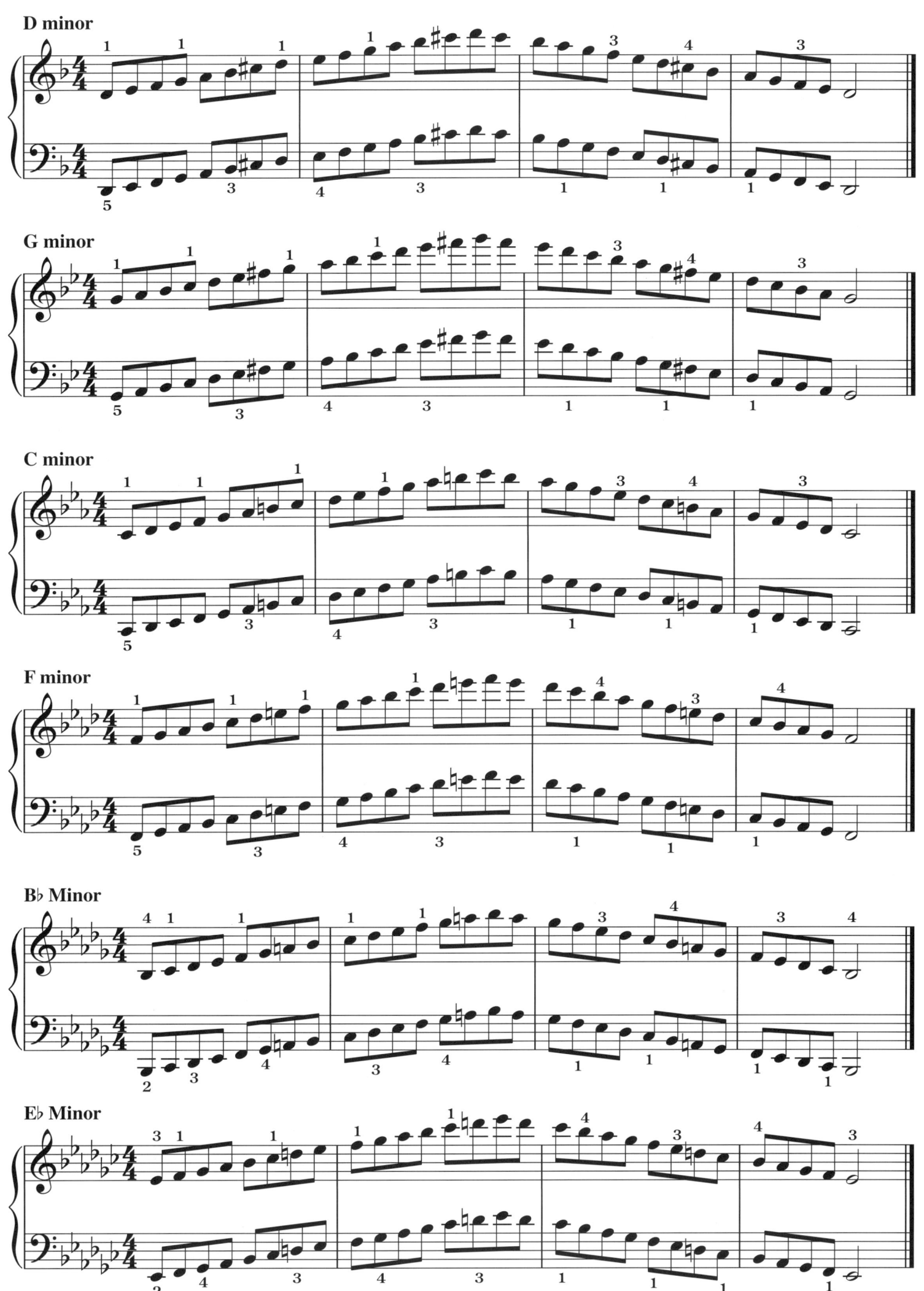

Primary Chord Progressions in Three Positions (Major Keys)

C Major

G Major

D Major

A Major

E Major

B Major

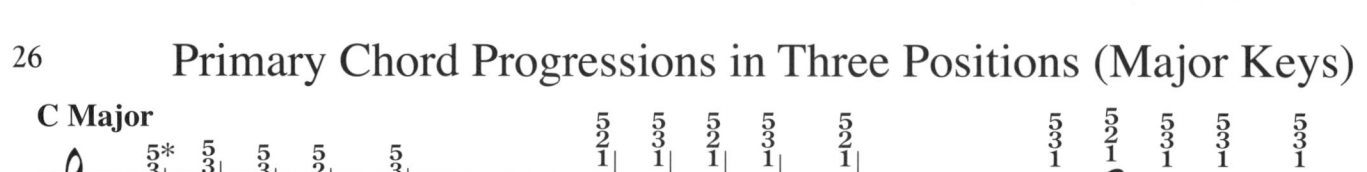

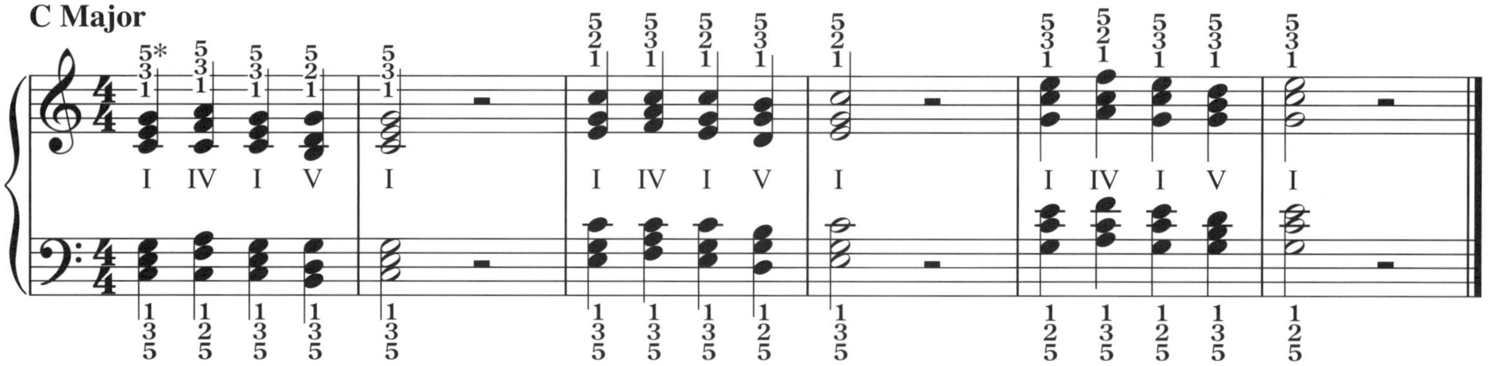

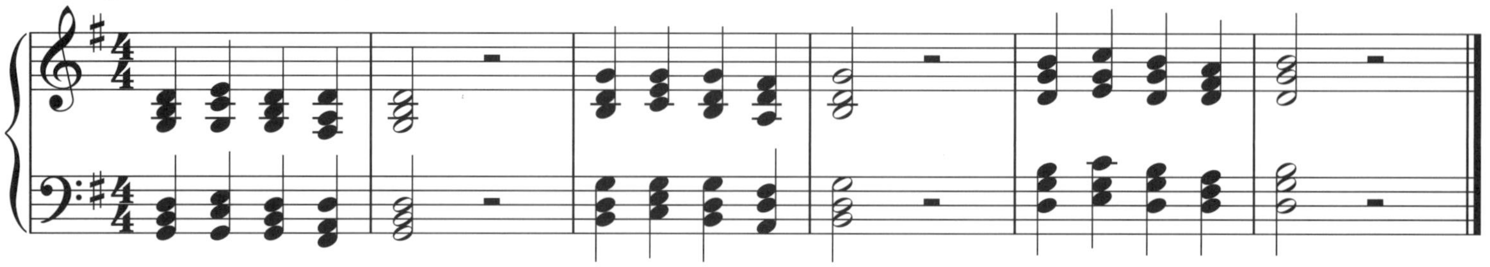

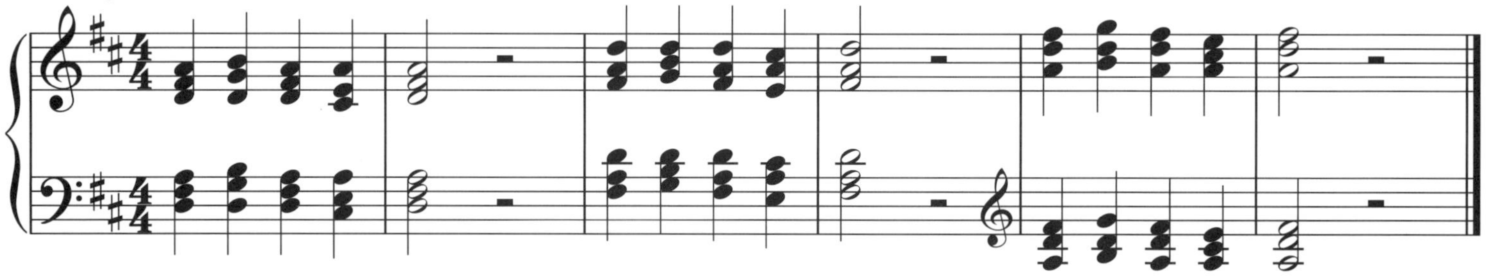

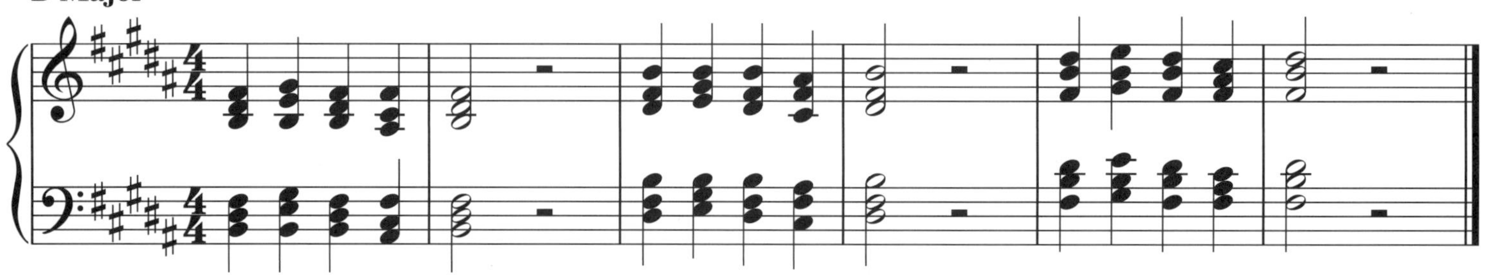

*Fingering is the same in every key.

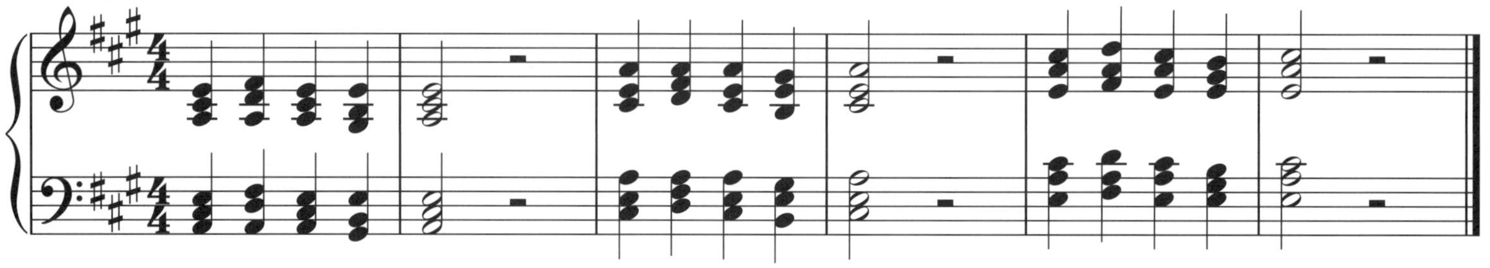

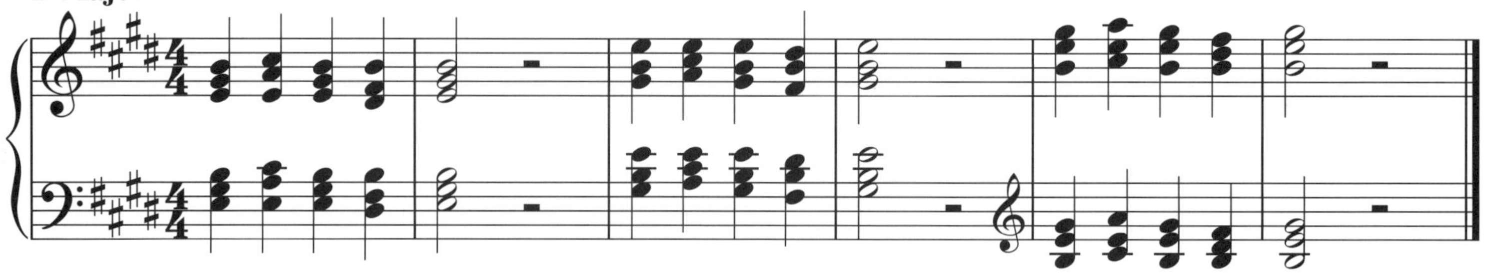

28

Primary Chord Progressions in Three Positions (Minor Keys)

Tonic Chord Arpeggios (Major Keys)

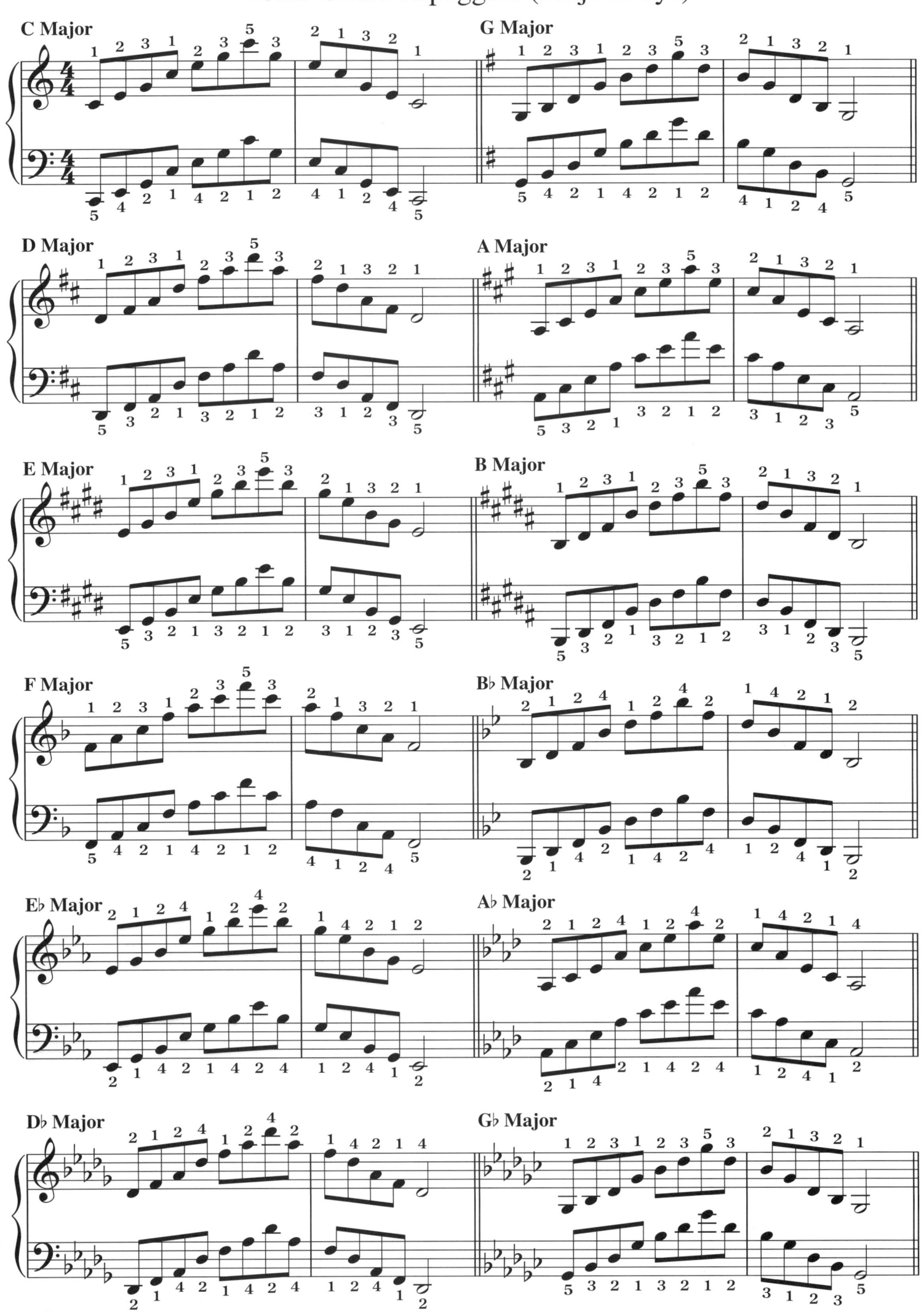

Tonic Chord Arpeggios (Minor Keys)

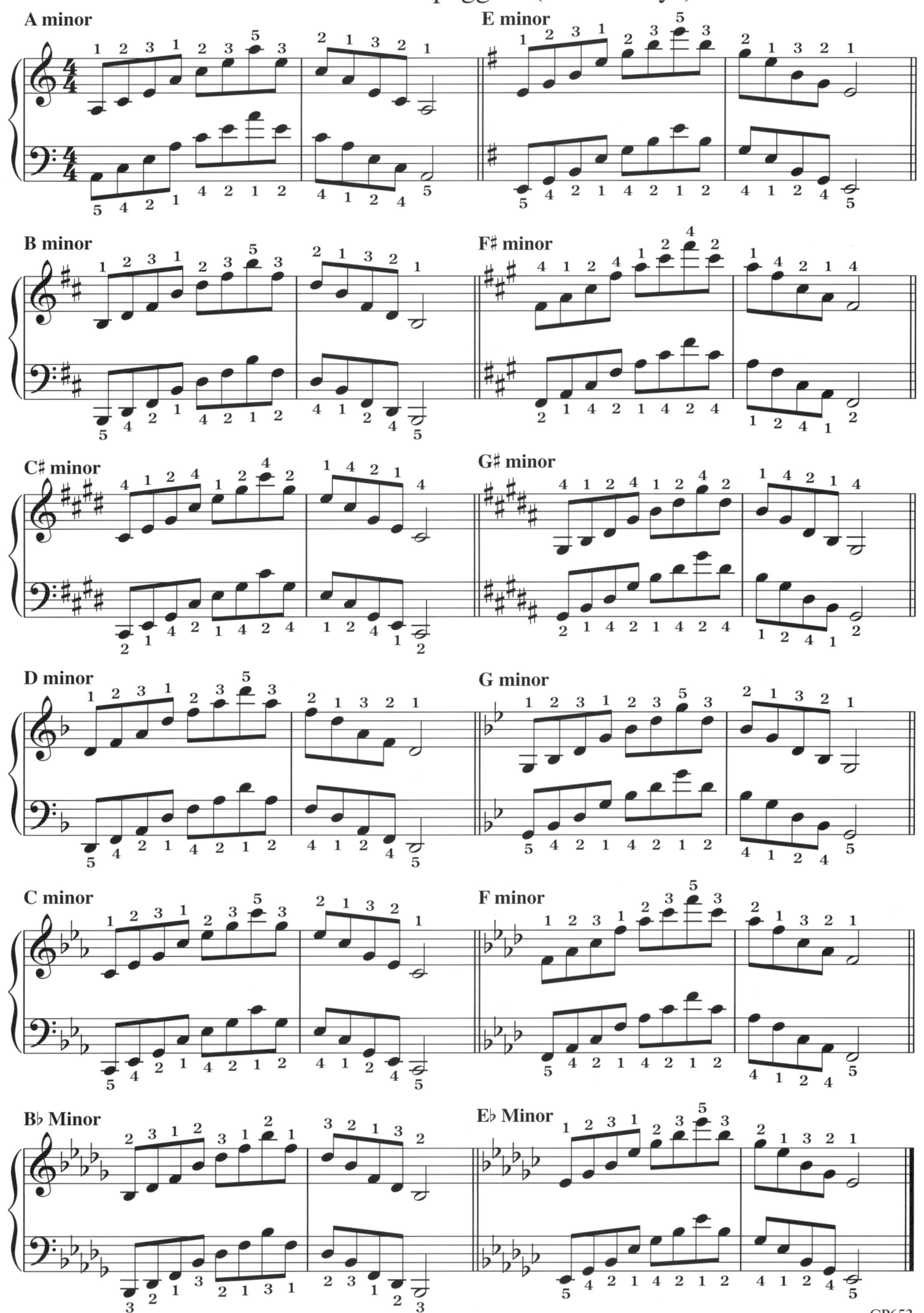

Chromatic Scales

1. **Contrary motion** starting a major 3rd apart, so the same fingers in each hand play at the same time. An alternate fingering for both hands is given in parentheses.

2. **Parallel motion** at the octave.

*When this scale is mastered, omit measure 5 and proceed directly from measure 4 to 6 without stopping.

**When this scale is mastered, repeat from the end of measure 9, rather than measure 10.